JOYFUL CRUELTY

ODÉON
JOSUÉ V. HARARI AND VINCENT DESCOMBES
General Editors

HERMENEUTICS AS POLITICS
Stanley Rosen

FAREWELL TO MATTERS OF PRINCIPLE
Philosophical Studies
Odo Marquard

THE LACANIAN DELUSION
François Roustang

A THEATER OF ENVY
William Shakespeare
René Girard

IN DEFENSE OF THE ACCIDENTAL
Philosophical Studies
Odo Marquard

PHILOSOPHY, POLITICS, AUTONOMY
Cornelius Castoriadis

JOYFUL CRUELTY
Clément Rosset

THE BAROMETER OF MODERN REASON
Vincent Descombes

COLD WAR CRITICISM
AND THE POLITICS OF SKEPTICISM
Tobin Siebers

Joyful Cruelty

Toward a Philosophy of the Real

CLÉMENT ROSSET

Edited and Translated by
David F. Bell

New York   Oxford
OXFORD UNIVERSITY PRESS
1993

Oxford University Press

Oxford   New York   Toronto
Delhi   Bombay   Calcutta   Madras   Karachi
Kuala Lumpur   Singapore   Hong Kong   Tokyo
Nairobi   Dar es Salaam   Cape Town
Melbourne   Auckland   Madrid

and associated companies in
Berlin   Ibadan

Copyright © 1993 by Oxford University Press, Inc.

Published by Oxford University Press, Inc.,
200 Madison Avenue, New York, New York 10016

Library of Congress Cataloging-in-Publication Data
Rosset, Clément.
[Essays. English. Selections]
Joyful cruelty : toward a philosophy of the real / Clément Rosset,
edited and translated by David F. Bell.
p.   cm.—(Odéon)
ISBN 0-19-507741-5
ISBN 0-19-507991-4(pbk.)
Includes bibliographical references and index.
Contents: The overwhelming force—Notes
on Nietzsche—The cruelty principle.
1. Reality.
2. Nietzsche, Friedrich Wilhelm, 1844–1900.
3. Joy.
I. Title.
BD331.R6452513 1993
194—dc20   92-15354

1 3 5 7 9 8 6 4 2

Printed in the United States of America
on acid-free paper

Contents

Introduction
Of Silence and Insouciance in Philosophy
David F. Bell

"When it comes to philosophy, the worst is often
probable."
—L.-M. Vacher, *Pour un matérialisme vulgaire*

After such a polite answer, my philosophy
counsels me to be silent and inquire no further,
especially since in certain cases, as the saying
suggests, one *remains* a philosopher only by—
being silent.
—Nietzsche, *Human, All Too Human*

There are many ways to describe Clément Rosset's philosophical project, but a first attempt might be to say that he is searching for a way to
be properly *idiotic*—on the condition, of course, that we understand
the term in a certain manner. Although it is normally pejorative, it can
paradoxically become a compliment, especially if it is proffered in
judgment by the typical philosopher appraising Rosset's work, for
Rosset has little positive to say himself concerning much of the philosophical tradition that defines our approach to the world. He would
almost certainly adhere to the remark made by Laurent-Michel Vacher
which serves as an epigraph. If one gives philosophy and philosophers
half a chance, they almost invariably tend toward the worst excesses.
More specifically, the probability is very high that they will devise an
approach to reality and the world which in fact turns away from the
world, occults it, and replaces it with a representation that supplants it
and supposedly expresses its higher truth. Faced with this betrayal of
the real, Rosset favors idiocy in its etymological sense, that is, *idiotes,*
an approach which is simple, particular, unique, and refuses all dou-
bling. This condemnation of much of the Western philosophical tradition is the result of abundant reflection upon that tradition and a
diagnosis of its problems. For Rosset there are ultimately two strains

in the history of philosophy. On the one hand, there is a speculative trend that finds its origin in Platonic philosophy and has been dominant from the very beginning. On the other hand, a second more or less suppressed current contests the illusions perpetrated by the speculative tradition, attempting instead to bring humanity face to face with the brutally chaotic nature of the real, its disorder and lack of meaning. Names such as Lucretius, Montaigne, Pascal, and Nietzsche surface as symbolic and effective illustrators of this second current.

How has the speculative tradition led philosophy astray and why has it done so? Quite simply put, the world, that which exists, holds absolutely no consolation for human beings, remarks Rosset in "The Overwhelming Force," the first of the three essays in the present volume. Faced with the meaninglessness of the world—the real, as Rosset calls it—the individual most often quakes and turns away. The experience of the real is literally unbearable, and philosophy has traditionally come to the rescue to save humanity from meaninglessness, to create the illusion of a truth which would remove us from the suffering necessarily entailed by an encounter with the real. Small wonder that speculative philosophies have regularly triumphed since the Greeks, for they offer consolation from the desolation of the real. That solace is false, however, and there have been a few lucid philosophers who have regularly countered speculation by resolutely calling us back to reality. Speculative philosophy cannot allow such incursions and has customarily relegated them to domains which are not considered a part of the noble philosophical tradition: Montaigne writes essays, Pascal leaves only fragments, Nietzsche is no more than a literary figure who prefers aphorism to argument, and so on.

Part of Rosset's project, then, involves a rereading of certain texts in the philosophical tradition. But that is certainly not his primary purpose, just as he himself would claim that the activity of critique is not the fundamental driving force of Nietzsche's philosophy. What Rosset invariably attempts to do in his thought is to provoke an encounter with the real, a moment of recognition during which his interlocutor might suddenly face the fact that all we have is the real and nothing more. Since that confrontation implies the recognition of the world in the absence of all mediation, it also intimates that philosophy can have no pretensions to interpret the confrontation, neither to mediate it nor to mitigate its effects. A philosophy which could fulfill such a draconian requisite for effacement would be perilously close to silence. What Rosset says of tragic discourse in a discussion devoted to the logic of the tragic could very well apply to philosophical discourse: "Logically, tragic discourse could, even should, stop here—with silence. . . . To make this silence continue to speak presupposes that one possesses a magic word, one which knows how to speak without saying anything, to think without conceiving of anything, to reject all ideology without itself being engaged in any ideology."[1] Truly to bring someone face to face with the real without flinching would necessitate avoiding representations of it in language. Only then would all temptation to turn away from the real be removed. Thus the true philosopher must be circumspect and must speak without affirming, with a voice that somehow confronts the difficulty of an essential link to silence. He or she must think without attempting to create or impose dogmatic conceptions, with a thought that has a lightness and perpetual movement about it.

Much of Rosset's recent reflection remains at the boundaries of this problem. The third essay of the present collection, "The Cruelty Principle," has much to say concerning the definition of the philosopher's predicament in the face of the need to speak in this strange half-voice bordering on silence. It sets out to define the limits of philosophical thought and arrives at the idea that philosophy is first and foremost a minimalist enterprise. The position which should be espoused by the philosopher is that of the minimal possible postulation: elaborate philosophical systems always overstep the boundaries of philosophical propriety, constructing schemes whose abstraction causes one to lose sight of the world. The consequence of such a decision is that Rosset considers materialist philosophies, those of Epicurus and Lucretius in particular, to be the best one can do in philosophy. Not that these doctrines hold any particular interest as assertive formulations; nothing could be more simplistic than the claims they make. The interest they do contain is to be found in their hygienic nature, in their knack of revealing the inherently empty speculation of other philosophical positions formulated by turning away from the real and conjecturing all manner of mediating principles. But is it really hygienic to turn people away from illusions which shelter them from the real? In some

absolute sense this is a dangerous activity. Few individuals are capable
of surviving the shock resulting from the recognition of the meaninglessness of the real. In fact, concludes Rosset, philosophy is very much
like medicine. Medicine has never really contributed anything except
to those who are already fundamentally healthy. Likewise, true philosophical ideas have never had a positive effect on anyone other than
those who already knew more or less what philosophy had to teach
them, namely, that there is no escape from the real. The shock of
therapy will kill those who are actually sick, just as the shock of the
real pushes those who never suspected they were living in illusion over
the brink into madness and suicide.

It is clear that Rosset is bent on puncturing all the pretensions that
have accompanied the so-called noble activity of philosophy. One cannot turn to philosophy to interpret the real; one has no recourse but to
confront it and to recognize its brutal nature. But then what should be
one's reaction when faced with the real? Are we condemned to a
bleakly pessimistic outlook on life? In other words, from a moral point
of view, how are we to live this life if there is no meaning to it?
Nothing could be more foreign to Rosset's approach than pessimism
in the face of this dilemma. Pessimism is, in fact, simply a surreptitious
approbation of the optimistic approach to life, the approach which
suggests that there is a meaning and a pattern that organizes the real.
The pessimist is one who rejects the real not simply because it is too
cruel but also, and more fundamentally, because he or she believes that
there could be something better, something other than the real. This
something other never materializes, of course; it is simply one of the
many illusions of potential order and signification manipulated by
those who refuse to face the fact of meaninglessness. If neither optimism nor pessimism is permissible, then precisely what attitude is
authorized or even possible at the moment when one finally faces the
real? Rosset calls the healthy reaction to the real *joy*. This is undoubtedly a paradoxical statement if one understands joy in its banal and
quotidian sense. As "The Overwhelming Force" explains, however,
joy is more than a simple emotion. It can never be fully explained as a
reaction to a particular event or thing; it always contains something
more. It overshoots its mark and somehow puts the person who experiences it in contact with a general approbation of the real in all its

chaotic and cruel presence. Joy is related to the Nietzschean embrace of life and to the Pascalian intervention of divine grace. In a situation in which there would seem to be no possible means of surviving the confrontation with the real, where suicide looks to be the only possible response, suddenly approbation emerges in the form of joy.

Joy reaches beyond the pale of mere emotion; it is a moral reaction of approbation produced by the recognition that occurs when one lays aside all mediation between oneself and the real. But it is also a veritable epistemological necessity and tool. No one who has not known the joyful approbation of the real can ultimately *know* the real. The reason is simple enough. Those who have not experienced that joyful approbation have of necessity turned away from the real, pulled back from it in horror and suffering. Thus they cannot pretend to experience it fully because they cannot bear the suffering it provokes. One knows the real only to the extent that one apprehends the bliss of approbation for all that exists, only to the extent that joy has intervened to keep one ever focused on the real alone, on the world as it is and not as it might be (and yet never will be). In speaking of joy as an instrument of knowledge of the world, one is never far from the Nietzschean gay science.

It seems almost inevitable, in fact, that Rosset's thought would have to undergo the trial, confront the measure of Nietzschean philosophy. Recent readers of his work tend to connect him to Nietzsche for better or worse. Jacques Bouveresse writes in his monograph on patterns of postmodern thought, *Rationalité et cynisme:* "Among the innumerable commentators and continuers whom Nietzsche's writings have elicited in France, I personally see only Rosset who has really understood and developed the most evident and yet the most difficult aspect of his lesson to assimilate. . . ."[2] By contrast, Laurent-Michel Vacher, who finds much inspiration in Rosset's work, balks at the Nietzschean airs he sees it assuming at certain moments, referring, for example, to Rosset's "nietzschéisme de mauvais aloi"—his debased Nietzscheism.[3] It is for this reason that the second essay of the present collection, "Notes on Nietzsche," must almost of necessity be included in any volume which aims to introduce Rosset's thought. Not only is Rosset often connected to Nietzsche, but, in addition, much of what has passed for postmodern thought in France over the past decade and a half has been explicitly located in what has been proclaimed (generally by the participants themselves) a Nietzschean trajectory. Is Rosset simply one more postmodern thinker inspired, albeit perhaps incorrectly, by Nietzsche's example? Although colloquia and books on Nietzsche have multiplied at a prodigious rate, one of the main characteristics of such activities in Rosset's view is that instead of attempting to understand Nietzsche's thought on its own terms, they have invariably led to the annexation of his work to the intellectual trend of the moment. One is thus left with a situation in which Nietzsche's thought and philosophical accomplishments are just as depreciated by his postmodern supporters and admirers as they were by his contemporaries, who bore the first shock of his fulminating, argumentative style. Certainly, states Rosset, it is no longer fashionable to claim, as did a previous generation of critics, that Nietzsche's ideas are wrong. It is much more "modern" to assert that his contribution to philosophy was precisely to mock it, to pretend to formulate ideas when in fact he was intent on debasing and destroying philosophy entirely. A cleverly turned argument, according to Rosset, but one which is even more pernicious for an understanding of Nietzsche's thought than that of the preceding generation because it succeeds in summarily dismissing any possible accomplishments Nietzsche may have made in the domain of philosophy.

To devise an approach to Nietzsche thus implies an effort to wrest control of his thought from those who have reveled in distorting it, to separate oneself from the self-proclaimed Nietzscheans. Rather than undertake an exegesis in traditional terms to accomplish this break, however, Rosset proceeds to reformulate a perspective on Nietzsche that concentrates on one fundamental notion from which all the rest will follow. What is crucial to Nietzschean thought is what Rosset calls *beatitude*. This is another way of expressing the approbation of the real, of refusing to speak about another "truer" world beyond what exists here and now. Everything in Nietzsche follows from this principle and this epistemological attitude—the whole gamut of his thought from the centrality of music to the mysterious theme of the eternal return. Those who have worked so hard to annex Nietzsche to the various projects of postmodernism have neglected Nietzschean beatitude and wrongly attributed to Nietzschean an attitude of pure refusal and critique.

The gay science, beatitude, joy: these descriptions of the perspective the philosopher must adopt toward the real are characteristic of Rosset's thought. The lesson of Nietzsche's philosophy is one of attitude and approach: it goes beyond the Nietzschean critique of the philosophical tradition. Fundamentally Rosset is in search of a philosophy that would be *tolerant,* refusing to believe that philosophy is an oppositional field of competing systems or ideas. Ideas are not opposed to one another, Rosset maintains; they are different from one another. In other words, they do not enter into a life-and-death struggle with one another; rather, they are exposed to the play of contradiction and testing. Philosophical ideas are propositions, thoughts put forth in an arena for discussion and debate. And because they are propositions in the full sense of the term, formulations set forth experimentally and with an open mind, they cannot be considered certain or true. Uncertainty and doubt, then, are what makes philosophical ideas intriguing and keeps them alive, for the ultimate philosophical trial, the act of doubting, always triumphs against any idea that is advanced as an absolute truth. The Cartesian gesture remains as effective against truth claims now as when Descartes first devised it. But doubt is paradoxically ineffective against ideas that are doubtful; it cannot undermine ideas that are presented as uncertain from the outset. This implies that the philosopher is not an author in the etymological sense of the term, for the philosopher does not guarantee the authority of the ideas he or she advances. Since the philosopher knows that there is no ultimate meaning to the world, any attempted description of meaning is not to be taken completely seriously and so can coexist with other uncertain propositions about lived experience. To say without saying means to postulate without affirming, to propose without insisting, to escape the trial of doubt by situating one's activity on doubtful terrain from the start. A proposition interrupts the becoming of the real only for a moment; it cannot definitively halt that becoming. The philosopher is thus as far removed as possible from the fanatic, who so believes in the certainty and truth of what he or she proposes that there is no choice but to try to impose his or her idea upon everyone else.

At first glance one might be tempted to say that Rosset's thought is characteristic in certain ways of familiar poststructuralist modes of dealing with meaning. The poststructuralist critique of structuralism

took the form of attempts to undo representation because poststruc-
turalists claimed that a certain stability of representation—and therefore a certain faith in the traditional belief in meaning and truth—
could be found at the heart of even the most iconoclastic acts of the
structuralist enterprise. But Rosset would undoubtedly claim that this
attempt to destabilize representation and the structures of meaning it
implies was not radical enough. The notion of deferral, whether in the
image of the labyrinth or in the "illusionism" of those whom Rosset
calls the "modern Hegelians" (Bataille, Derrida, and others), still re-
tains a logic of meaning which suggests that if we accomplish a sufficiently thorough working through of the concept, we might find an
ultimate signification after all. Nor is the more ironic postmodern
perspective on meaning, the celebration of its demise in a mixing of
styles and metaphors, in a rediscovery of classical representational
styles that are no longer attached to their contexts and become empty
rhetorical figures playing endlessly and eclectically with one another,
radical enough.[4] Playing with meaning, particularizing and multiply-
ing it in an attempt to undo it by a proliferating liberation still would
remain for Rosset, I think, too attached to its seduction. The minimalist approach to what exists, the effort to encounter the real in the
absence of all mediation, precludes the kind of rhetorical trifling common in postmodern thought and demands instead a simple approach
toward and an approbation of the real that seems particularly difficult
for postmodern thought to imagine or accept.

What sets Rosset apart from certain postmodern trends in French
philosophy may be summed up by saying that he exudes a certain
insouciance. In order to define what is suggested by this term, it is
perhaps best to indicate what the attitude of insouciance is meant to
replace. For Rosset one of the fundamental problems of postmodern
attempts to radicalize philosophy is that they take the philosophical
tradition too seriously. In particular, they are too oblivious to the fact
that the best philosophers have always been the ones who have themselves been the most circumspect with regard to the ideas they propose. In a strange twist postmodern thinkers take the foremost texts of
the tradition even more seriously than did those who produced them.
Contemporary philosophy thus often appears to have nothing better
to do than endlessly interpret the texts of the philosophical tradition

with a critical but ever-present reverence. It revels in exegesis, totally oblivious to what exists. Rosset's opposition to this tendency should not be taken as a gesture against learning and culture; indeed it is a posture that could only be adopted by one who is himself thoroughly versed in the culture being called into question. It stems instead from another and different vision of the destiny of philosophy, one that makes of it an exercise in preparation for the confrontation with what is, an activity which should under no circumstances mitigate that confrontation. Perhaps even more essentially, contemporary philosophers simply take themselves too seriously. Rosset's attitude recalls, in another key and in a different context, a remark by Peter Sloterdijk concerning the activity of critique: "Recent ideology critique already appears in respectable garb, and in Marxism and especially in psychoanalysis it has even put on suit and tie so as to completely assume an air of bourgeois respectability. It has given up its life as satire, in order to win its position in books as 'theory.' "[5] Even the apparent playfulness of postmodern thinkers cannot mask an ill-defined and poorly analyzed feeling of respect and reverence for the very activity in which they are engaged. The result of such an attitude is a certain grandiloquence in philosophical discourse which is never far from pedantry, platitude, and repetition. Philosophers are willing to undergo every ordeal with the exception of the ordeal of insouciance, as Rosset puts it in "Notes on Nietzsche." Anyone who fundamentally believes that the real is all that counts must also understand that philosophical activity cannot replace the real, cannot pretend to position itself in a hierarchy above what exists in the world.

Once again, however, a great deal of care must be exercised in understanding the precise nature of the insouciance at stake here. It may appear that the philosopher who maintains such an attitude has abandoned all semblance of worldly concern, when, on the contrary, he or she is the only one who demonstrates a proper concern for and recognition of the real. The casual reformer, who has inherited the progressive ideology formulated in the eighteenth century and disseminated in gradually more vulgarized terms ever since, and who maintains that "we can change the world," has not undergone the ordeal of the real, has refused to accept the cruelty of its unmediated disorder and chaos, has turned away from it in an effort to build another world

when all we shall ever have is this one. Only the peculiar combination
of joy, approbation, and insouciance allows access to what exists. Even
Rosset's style of argument exudes this paradoxical stance. Although he
often refers to and quotes from philosophical texts, he is just as much
at ease with literary texts, sometimes obscure, or with music, often
outside the so-called mainstream of the musical tradition, if these
capture the attitude and sensations he is seeking to expound. A Mau-
passant short story or a scene by Proust can come closer to conveying
the salient aspects of the confrontation with the real than any abstract
philosophical discourse, as can a Buster Keaton film or a piece of music by de Falla. It is almost as if the surprise encounter with the real
were also—and just as important—the product of a series of surprise
encounters with the most varied cultural sources. Rosset has the gift of
the essayist, which allows him to vault from one cultural manifestation
to the next, proposing ideas only to bifurcate toward something else
before any idea is affirmed too heavy-handedly. If there is a little of
Nietzsche in Rosset, there is also a little of Montaigne, a kind of
sensual pleasure in the multifaceted manifestations of what exists. He
most certainly adheres to their project of embracing the world in its
every aspect, their refusal of all semblances of reality that would mask
its character. Like the texts of Lucretius, Montaigne, Pascal, and Nietzsche, Rosset's writings reach out to those who are healthy enough to
eschew illusion and live this life: his diagnosis is therapeutic only for
the strongest at heart.

Works by Clément Rosset

La Philosophie tragique. Paris: Presses Universitaires de France, 1960

Le Monde et ses remèdes. Paris: Presses Universitaires de France, 1964

Lettre sur les chimpanzées: plaidoyer pour une humanité totale. Paris: Gallimard, 1965

Schopenhauer, philosophe de l'absurde. Paris: Presses Universitaires de France, 1967

L'Esthétique de Schopenhauer. Paris: Presses Universitaires de France, 1969

Logique du pire: éléments pour une philosophie tragique. Paris: Presses Universitaires de France, 1971

L'Anti-nature: éléments pour une philosophie tragique. Paris: Presses Universitaires de France, 1973

Le Réel et son double: essai sur l'illusion. Paris: Gallimard, 1976

Le Réel: traité de l'idiotie. Paris: Minuit, 1977

L'Objet singulier. Paris: Minuit, 1979

La Force majeure. Paris: Minuit, 1983

Le Philosophe et les sortilèges. Paris: Minuit, 1985

Le Principe de cruauté. Paris: Minuit, 1988

Principes de sagesse et de folie. Paris: Minuit, 1991

Matière d'art: hommages. Paris: Passeur, 1992

JOYFUL CRUELTY

=1=

The Overwhelming Force

The gods have hidden what keeps men alive.
—Hesiod, *Works and Days*

One of the surest identifying properties of joy is its totalitarian nature, to use an expression with disturbing resonances in many respects. Joy is an all-or-nothing proposition. It is either complete or nonexistent (and I would add, in anticipation of my argument to follow, that there is no joy which is not simultaneously complete and in a certain way nonexistent). The joyous person is filled with joy for this or that particular reason, of course. But if one digs a little more deeply, one quickly discovers that a person is filled with joy also for this or that other reason, or for yet another reason, and so on endlessly. The rejoicing is not particular but general; the person is "joyous with all joys," *omnibus laetitiis laetum,* as a lover fulfilled puts it in a play by the Latin dramatist Trabea, partially quoted by Cicero. A penetrating remark, although everything concerning the context in which it was situated remains a mystery. What such a remark suggests can be expressed something like this: there is in joy a mechanism of approval which tends to overshoot the particular object that first caused it and to affect all objects indifferently, resulting ultimately in an affirmation of the jubilant character of existence in general. Joy thus appears to be a sort of blank check granted to anything and everything, like an unconditional approbation of every form of existence past, present, or future.

One curious consequence of this totalitarianism: the truly joyous

3

person is recognizable by the fact that he is incapable of saying exactly why he is joyous, of furnishing the precise reason for present satisfaction. He would have far too much to say in general on this point—far too much to say—while finding nothing in particular to adduce. When he has finished praising the merits of different French wines (a whole lifetime would not suffice to complete even this short chapter), the merits of Greek or Italian landscapes, those of the morning and the evening, everything would remain to be said about the charm of existence—everything or nearly everything, infinity minus one or two elements. What he would say would also be insufficient, because his joy can be explained by no precise fact—on the one hand because of the principle which prohibits general praise from being founded on a single fact, and on the other for the simple reason that in any case there is no object on which praise can be founded, all such objects invariably succumbing to the corrosive effect of analysis and reflection. There is no worldly object which a lucid examination cannot definitively reveal to be laughable and unworthy of attention, if only from the point of view of its fragile constitution—I mean of its simultaneously ephemeral and minuscule position in the infinity of time and space. The strange thing is that joy remains, nonetheless, although suspended in thin air and deprived of all ground. This is in fact the extraordinary privilege of joy, the aptitude to persevere even though its cause is lost and condemned. It possesses the quasi-feminine art of surrendering to no argument, of blithely ignoring the most obvious adversity as well as the most flagrant contradictions. Joy has in common with femininity the fact that it remains indifferent to every objection. An incomprehensible faculty of persistence permits joy to survive its own death, to continue to strut about as if nothing had happened. It's a bit like a worm which, even though it is cut into two or four parts, nevertheless continues to move and to progress toward its unknown goal, or like the miraculous mandarin, put to music by Béla Bartók, who cannot be killed no matter how many times he is stabbed. The insistence of joy reveals a radical and characteristic disproportion between all profound rejoicing and the object which gives rise to it, or more precisely its *pretext.* Joy thus always constitutes a sort of "over and above," an effect which is supplementary and disproportionate relative to its real cause and which multiplies this or that satisfaction pertaining to any well-defined reason. This over and above, moreover, is precisely what the joyous person is incapable of expressing, much less of explaining. Joy is an inexpressible hypothesis, in the same manner and for the same reasons that the hypothesis of the One as Plato dissects it in the *Parmenides* is inexpressible, obliged as we are to say everything about it, which is impossible (and contradictory in the case of the One), or to say nothing about it, which leads us to situate joy at the margin if not totally outside of all that exists and is sayable (just as the One is separated from being, according to the first hypothesis of the *Parmenides*). Caught between too much to say and too little, the approbation of life remains forever inexpressible. Any attempt to express it necessarily dissolves into a more or less inaudible and unintelligible stammering.

One could immediately say—and this is the first of three objections to which I would like to respond before proceeding—that this sort of vague yearning which is joy thus defined corresponds point by point to its exact opposite, namely, the romantic vague yearning [*vague à l'âme*] which inclines toward melancholy and sadness. It would be insufficient simply to protest that at stake here are two different and diametrically opposed spiritual dispositions because the formal resemblance is so evident that it cannot be ignored. Just as the joyful person is incapable of expressing the reason for his joy and the nature of what overwhelms him, so also the melancholy person does not know how to identify precisely the reason for his sadness or the nature of what he is lacking—except to repeat with Baudelaire that his melancholy is infinite and that what he is lacking does not belong to the register of things which exist. If, however, the world as a whole is as indescribable as the group of things situated outside the world—*anywhere out of the world*, as Baudelaire puts it—it differs from them nonetheless in one major characteristic, which is naturally its *existence*. Thus the fundamental difference between the vague yearning of the romantic and that of the joyful person is that the first fails to describe what does not exist, while the second fails to describe what does exist. In other words, joy is always somehow engaged with the real, while sadness unceasingly confronts the unreal—and that is its specific misfortune. Montherlant illustrates this underlying truth when he writes, in *Pitié pour les femmes:* "Don't you see, there is only one way to love women, and that is with love. . . . Everything else—friendship, esteem, intellectual sympathy—is a phantom in the absence of love, a cruel phantom, because a phantom is truly cruel. One can always work things out when it's just a question of reality."[1]

Second objection: as it is normally considered, joy does not consist of a rejoicing lacking all reason, like a motor racing in neutral, as it were, but results from the satisfaction of a precise expectation, from the obtainment of a desired and defined object. How could one be happy about nothing, joyous for naught? Let me point out, however, that such a case, as rare and extraordinary as it may seem, is far from being unheard of. There are outbursts of joy independent of any cause, paroxysms of euphoria perfectly incompatible with conscious thought when consciousness can decipher in its personal horoscope only grounds for sadness and discouragement. "Merely to breathe was an enjoyment, and I derived positive pleasure even from many of the legitimate sources of pain," writes Poe in "The Man of the Crowd."[2] Another striking example of this contradictory euphoria may be found in one of Michelet's childhood memories:

> I remember a moment of supreme misfortune, amidst present privations, fears of the future, when the enemy was at our doorstep (1814!) and my own enemies were taunting me daily. That day, a Thursday morning, with no heat despite the snow on the ground, I collected my thoughts, not knowing if there would be bread in the evening. Everything seemed finished for me, but I had within myself, in the absence of any smattering of religious hope, a pure stoic sentiment, and thus I struck my oak table (which I have always kept) with my freezing hand and felt a virile joy of youth and hope.[3]

Such texts remind us that joy, like the rose of which Angelus Silesius speaks in *The Cherubic Wanderer,* can on occasion do without any *raison d'être.* They also suggest that in the most unfavorable situation, in the absence of all reasonable grounds for rejoicing, the essence of joy can perhaps best be grasped.

The fact remains naturally that everyday joy is commonly linked to a cause, to a reason for satisfaction. On this point it is enough to consult the Delphic charioteer and his mysterious smile, more jubilant still than any frank and flaunted joy: "I will make of it no great matter," he appears to be thinking, "but it is a fact that I am not unhappy to have triumphed." This subdued rejoicing is the common distinguishing characteristic of all motivated joy, strong in its indisputable triumph but also limited and particular. If it is certain, however, that a reason for satisfaction can provoke joy in the same way that opportunity can create the thief, one might say, it does not necessarily follow that joy thus obtained is completely defined by the favorable circumstance that gave rise to it. For under the circumstances, the cause is inferior to the effect that it creates, a little like what happens in family quarrels when the avowed reasons for hostility which bring about the crisis in the first place—an inheritance dispute, for example—only bare for all to see an accumulation of hatred which preexisted the direct confrontation and would have continued to exist without it, masked by politeness and declarations of friendship. It is commonly said in such cases that the parties began to detest one another for reasons pertaining to money. The truth is the opposite, however: they began to confront one another on questions of money because they detested one another. It is not the monetary dispute which provokes the hatred but hatred which provokes the monetary dispute. In the same manner, the accumulation of love of which joy consists is ultimately foreign to any cause which provokes it, even if it sometimes happens that joy becomes manifest only at the moment of this or that particular satisfaction. This is why one can speak here of a cause which is inferior to its effect, although the expression seems to fly in the face of logic. The cause does not produce the "effect" but merely reveals it, as it were; the effect is a fact existing before the cause. On this point one must concede what Spinoza says in the *Ethics:* the only affection is joy (and its opposite, sadness); any other affection is but a modification of this fundamental affection as it is subjected to the play of chance and fortune. Thus, love for a person is defined by Spinoza as a simple interference between joy and the other: "*Love* is nothing but joy accompanied by the idea of an external cause."4 In the same way, hatred is sadness accompanied by the idea of an external cause.

Joy thus appears independent of any appropriate circumstance which might provoke it (as it is independent of any appropriate circumstance which might thwart it). In relation to any reason for satisfaction, including, I insist, the set of all reasons which can make it burst forth on any particular occasion, joy always appears to be a type of gratification, indeed that extra bliss of which the Gospels speak in relation to terrestrial joys given in recompense to those who have refused them while banking on the beyond: "Everything else will be given you in addition"; you will inherit both the heavens and the earth. For my part, I shall observe here only that the experience of joy contains something which exceeds all considerations that would attempt to explain it by exposing only its "content." No object alone could make one joyful. Or, rather, it so happens at times that some object can make one joyous, but the paradoxical fate of such an object is thus to give more than it really gives, more than it "objectively" possesses. It is said that the most beautiful woman in the world can give only what she has. In other words, it is vain to expect of reality more than it can give: most assuredly a correct statement, but only up to a certain point because it is contradicted by joy, which easily gives rise to this apparently impossible performance. It is not that joy asks of reality more than it can offer but that it obtains more than could reasonably be expected. To illustrate this point I would once again invoke the Delphic charioteer, winner of the chariot race in the Pythian Games. His smile is eloquent but also rather complex. In it, most assuredly, is much happiness, but at the same time a prudence and circumspection which reflect something other than the simple pleasure of having won. Naturally one can interpret this reserve in multiple ways. What follows is a psychological interpretation, automatic but not particularly convincing: one is dealing with a well-educated young man, who has the modesty to minimize his victory under public scrutiny, a public which will admire the winner that much more, and who behaves the same way toward the losers, thus increasing their resentment. And then there is the Hegelian interpretation: Greek serenity never attains perfect satisfaction, always feeling a secret nostalgia when forced to content itself with its own *Dasein*, which, according to Hegel, turns out to be incapable of assuming totally the spiritual destiny of man. I would opt for quite a different interpretation of the charioteer's smile, seeing in it the gravity belonging to joy as Greek sculpture expressed it many times. More particularly, in the case of the charioteer it depicts the emotion of a man who had prepared himself for the eventuality of a certain happiness and suddenly finds himself confronted with something quite different and also more intense. Not only is his satisfaction not imperfect; better still, it is more perfect than any expectation. I would readily say that the sculptor's chisel captured

the look of the charioteer at the precise instant when he ceased thinking about the happiness of his victory to think about something else
entirely: the general joy which consists in living, in realizing that the
world exists and that one is a part of it.

This passage from the particular to the general, from a simple bliss to
a sort of cosmic well-being, is very present in the rejoicing par excellence
of living species, namely, sexuality. In the case of sexual pleasure and in
the indiscernible joy it provokes, it becomes manifest—even though this
observation applies to any form of rejoicing, albeit to a lesser degree—
that pleasure is not entirely defined by what the protagonists receive
from the act, nor by what the single protagonist receives if one is speaking of solitary pleasure. There is always a third term upon which this joy
has an effect: not only the interest of the species, linked to certain
circumstances favorable to mating, but, in addition, the general interest
of existence experienced by sexual pleasure in all its forms. Georges
Bataille, and before him Schopenhauer (although both draw consequences from this fact that are diametrically opposed to those I draw for
my part), profoundly discerned in sexual joy a rejoicing which utterly
exceeds the interests of the individual, of the moral as well as the physical person—the former having often been the loser in this affair and the
latter never the winner. Sexual joy is thus an effect which escapes its
cause, a profit which slips through the fingers of its supposed benefi-
ciary. Thus, there is an eventual disillusionment on the part of the
person who has invested heavily in this area; he never gets his just due.
But there is also a supreme jubilation in recovering much more than one
had invested. One can mention here the most common experience.
Sexual pleasure always reveals a remarkable shortfall between the anticipated pleasure and the pleasure actually obtained, a shortfall, moreover, that is recorded in everyday language which readily and correctly
declares that sexual pleasure transports one, in other words, it accom-
plishes a "transport," a displacement. A pleasure [*jouissance*][5] not simply more intense but of another order takes the place of the anticipated
pleasure, because it is no longer a certain body which appears to be the
source of pleasure but all bodies indiscriminately, and even the fact of
existence in general, suddenly felt to be universally desirable. What
happens at the moment of orgasm can thus be described as a passage
from the singular to the general, from the search for a particular plea-

sure to the obtaining of, if not a universal pleasure, at least one which is felt to be such. In the end the two are not that far apart because sexual pleasure, like the aesthetic pleasure analyzed by Kant in the *Critique of Judgment,* and like, moreover, pleasure taken in anything whatsoever, implies the idea of a legitimate pretension to a universal recognition, even if this unanimity has no chance of ever being realized concretely.

What I am saying concerning sexual rejoicing naturally applies only to cases of realized and successful orgasm. It often happens, as we all know, that sexual pleasure, far from leading to a general rejoicing, is, on the contrary, felt as a deception and leads to that characteristic sadness of which the Latin adage is representative, according to which every animal is rendered morose by the accomplishment of the sexual act: post coïtum omne animal triste. This morosity is made possible by the fact that the accomplishment of the sexual act does not automatically bring the accomplishment of sexuality in the widest and most rejoicing sense of the term. Orgasm in itself is a necessary but not a sufficient condition for sexual joy. This is why Freud is always right to distinguish between sexuality and the sexual act. Thus in a 1910 article he writes: "We use the word 'sexuality' in the same comprehensive sense as that in which the German language uses the word *lieben* [to love]. We have long known, too, that mental absence of satisfaction with all its consequences can exist where there is no lack of normal sexual intercourse; and as therapists we always bear in mind that the unsatisfied sexual trends (whose substitutive satisfactions in the form of nervous symptoms we combat) can often find only very inadequate outlets in coitus or other sexual acts."[6]

A third objection, apparently more worrisome than the two preceding ones, can be brought against the definition of joy as a universal rejoicing. The very idea of a passage toward the universal is suspicious in essence, assimilable to the process of fanaticism and proselytism whereby a belief is defended by the faithful only if it is in their view simultaneously susceptible to being imposed on the whole of humankind. The fact that any given sentiment can be valid for the person who feels it only if it involves willy-nilly all those who do not feel it is, as is well known, the eternal rule of fanaticism. It should be pointed out that fanaticism breeds on that eminently terroristic idea, presented over the past two centuries as eminently liberal and progressive, according to which all persons are like one another.[7] Nothing could be more disturbing, in fact, nor more dangerous for those who are the apparent beneficiaries than this avowal of universal similitude and fraternity. For it follows from the fact that so-and-so must be considered my fellow man that he must necessarily think what I think, consider good what I consider to be good, and if he objects, we will force him to open his eyes. This is why the fact of recognizing one's fellow man in someone else always constitutes less a favor than a constraint and a violent act. This is also why every manifestation of humanism verges on terrorism. Take, for example, the Declaration of the Rights of Man and other Immortal Principles which have had many occasions since their proclamation to demonstrate that if they were perhaps not all that immortal in the long run, they were, at least for the time being and while awaiting something better, passably deadly. It is evident, however, that this vice, inherent in totalitarianism in all its forms, is completely foreign to the generality of joy. What profoundly distinguishes ordinary totalitarianism from the "totalitarianism" of joy is that the former, unlike joy, which is content with its own faculty of approbation, exists only under the condition of and demand for approbation by the other. This difference may be explained essentially by the fact that the belief defended by totalitarianism is, unlike joy, not very consistent with itself. The extremely vague object to which it adheres with all its force can find serious consistency only via the mediation of a general consent, or one that is held to be such, which alone can give it an appearance of credibility, or rather an appearance of existence. This is precisely why totalitarianism spares no means to force such consent, consent being for it, strictly speaking, a question of life and death, the final instance deciding on its being or nonbeing. What totalitarianism expects from the verdict of the people is thus less a manifestation of truth than one of existence—not simply a formula like, "Since everyone believes it, it must be true," but also, more profoundly, "Since everyone believes it, then what I believe in is *something.*" In short, the doctrine which totalitarianism espouses is like an empty space which can be filled or satisfied only by a general consent on the part of the other, which is never fully realized. By contrast, joy is a plenitude which suffices unto itself and needs no external support in order to be.

One last remark before coming to the most crucial question: the joy of which I am speaking is completely indistinguishable from the joy of life [*joie de vivre*], from the simple pleasure of existing (even if an analysis of the latter reveals it to be a rather complex rejoicing, a pleasure rather in the fact that there is an existence in general than in the fact of any personal existence). That is certainly a cause for confusion, but a voluntary and deliberate confusion founded on the idea that there is no effective difference between joy and the joy of life, further, that there is no surer sign of joy than to be one and the same with the joy of life. There is a long philosophical tradition from Plato to Heidegger which has believed differently, considering, on the contrary, that there is no joy truly accessible to humanity unless one "goes beyond" the simple joy of life, distancing oneself from any object situated in existence, as heartening as that object may be. This thesis— and it would be ridiculous to say that it was erroneous, if only because of the number and quality of the people throughout the ages who have felt that it was true—is supported by the idea that there is no existing object that can be "objectively" held to be desirable, as I have stated. The consequence seems to be that joy, if it does not consist of an illusory rejoicing quickly contradicted by its very object, could only consist of an experience, mystic or metaphysical in nature, that has in fact been described by this or that theologian or philosopher—Pascal or Heidegger, for example, or Plato in the *Phaedrus,* assimilating the dying swan's song with a song of joy and deliverance. Very generally speaking, such joy appears a means of escaping the present in favor of a more permanent "presence," escaping fugitive existence in favor of an eternal being. What can be said here not against this thesis whose cogency I cannot discuss but in favor of the joy of life and its own cogency can be summarized by two major types of argument. The first, which is regularly used, appears rather specious, while the second, less often formulated, seems very solid and even decisive.

First argument: the joy of life consists of a compromise with life in a renunciation of all pretension toward duration in exchange for ephemeral joys that can be obtained from existence. The joy of life is thus only a surrogate for authentic joy, like physical love, which, if we are to believe Plato in the *Symposium,* is only a surrogate for love itself. And the perpetuation of the human species which it permits is only a sort of occasional immortality, a surrogate for the eternity of being. One can immediately grasp the weakness of this argument in favor of the joy of life, since it situates the joy of life in the register of resignation and of "for lack of something better," ultimately compromising with the adversary from the beginning to the point of admitting all his or her conclusions. This is thus an inadmissible, if not to say a suicidal, argument, but it is also a false argument which simultaneously exposes the substance of the second and only strong argument in favor of the joy of life in order to denounce it. For the analysis shows manifestly that the joy of life never aims for anything less than the stability and the perenniality of an imperishable and unaltering being. Quite the contrary: the joy of life breathes comfortably only in an ephemeral, perishable existence, always changing and desired as such. Such comfort can, of course, be considered paradoxical, suspected even of expressing a sort of heroic and masochistic madness. I believe, however, that this is not true in the least, and that the most common experience of joy testifies in favor of this habitual and quite earthly rejoicing. The savor of existence is that of time passing and changing, of the nonfixed, of what is never certain or complete. In this fluctuation, moreover, is found the best and the surest "permanence" of life. To have a taste for such a thing implies necessarily that one rejoices precisely in the fact that life is essentially both perishable and renewable, and this is a far cry from regretting an absence of stability and perenniality. The charm of autumn, for example, is related less to the fact that it is autumn than to the fact that it modifies summer before, in turn, finding itself modified by winter. And its real "being" consists precisely in the modification that it brings about. But one can hardly imagine what would make up the charm of autumn "in its essence," as the disciple of Plato might want to imagine it. I would add that an autumn in its essence, no matter how one might represent it, primarily and especially would not be very "autumnal." This goes to show that the charm of existence, far from being appreciated in proportion to a problematic participation in eternity, is measured, on the contrary, in proportion to its distance from being as it is conceived by ontologists and metaphysicians—like autumn, which exists if and only if there is no "being" of autumn. This is why Odysseus, on several occasions in the *Odyssey,* opposes the vigor of existence, no matter how fugitive

and miserable, to the pallor and inconsistency of immortality, no matter how glorious—immortality which Calypso offers him from the
very beginning of the epic but which he steadfastly refuses. In the same
vein he praises the posthumous immortality of Achilles only for ur-
banely courteous reasons when he encounters him by chance during a
visit to the underworld. Achilles interrupts him after the first compliment: "My lord Odysseus, . . . spare me your praise of Death. . . . I
would rather be a serf in the house of some landless man, with little
enough for himself to live on, than king of all these dead men that have
done with life."[8] In short, the simple fact of living is in itself a refusal
and refutation of being and its ontological attributes, immortality and
eternity. Naturally it does not follow from this incompatibility between life and being that the joy of life is the same as joy. To arrive at
this final equation I must add a third argument, taken from Spinoza,
according to which there is more "perfection"—that is, reality—in the
joy of life than in joy alone (if one considers joy an aiming for or a
vision of a being surpassing every form of existence). The joy of life is
present and complete, but joy is virtual and awaits its own fulfillment,
if not to say its own content. That is why all joy in my opinion consists
of the joy of life and of that alone.

The fact that simple existence is in itself a source of rejoicing, even
though at times its beneficiaries ignore it and may not even realize it, is
attested in addition by the observation of a very banal and quotidian
fact, one so widely occurring that it can be taken as exemplary. I mean
the extreme interest that most people have in the evocation of their
memories, or more precisely the desire to be exact that they demonstrate in this area, even though the memories in question present nothing particularly remarkable or joyful. Once existence simply happens,
it then becomes, as soon as those who were its participants or heroes
evoke it later on, a subject of interminable discussion and passionate
debate—a debate whose intensity seems all the more unusual in that
its stakes are for the most part rather minimal. Nothing, however, is
left to chance any longer. The smaller one's investment in what was
happening in the past when one was participating in the events, the
more one now refuses to hear that artichokes were served that day
when in fact one remembers excellent asparagus, or that the sky
cleared at the end of the day when in fact it became cloudy, that

someone telephoned when in fact, contrary to all expectations, he did
not call. One ought to inquire into the origins of such a lively interest
in the past, since when it was present, it was generally experienced as
indifferent, if not vaguely disagreeable. This fastidious character of
remembrance can only be interpreted as the mark of recognition, in
the double sense of the term, with respect to existence as such, of the
inherent interest of all existence whatever it may be. The exercise of
memory bears testimony in favor of existence and its prerogative, even
though it becomes conscious of this only after the fact. Its mania for
exactness, for conformity with past reality, acknowledges somewhat
late that "things which exist are important," to use [Paul] Claudel's
expression in *Le Pain dur*.

I should now like to examine the central paradox of joy, which I have
only sketched up to now. This paradox can be formulated briefly: joy is
an unconditional rejoicing for and with respect to existence, whereas
existence is anything but joyful and heartening if it is examined with all
the coldness and lucidity of rationality. It is doubtless not worthwhile
here to enter into the details of the givens which force thought, and have
always forced it, to decide against existence and to recognize in it an
indefensible and undesirable character. Let us simply recall that they
essentially come down to a lack of time and a fault of space. What comes
into existence, what its real "being" consists of, has no chance or possibility of lasting, just as it has no chance or possibility of occupying an
appreciable place in the infinity of space. This realization of the nothingness or near nothingness to which the most fascinating object is necessarily reduced is the *punctum pruriens* of philosophy, the painful place
among all painful places, the point where all thoughts come, strictly
speaking, to "rot." It constitutes the "sickness unto death" of which
Kierkegaard speaks, the thought which, century after century, has ship-
wrecked all attempts at philosophical lifesaving, by which I mean every
attempt to conciliate rationally the jubilatory exercise of life and the
recognition of the precariousness of existence. Before Nietzsche, Montaigne realized that therein lay the most dangerous thought, the evil that
was absolutely without remedy and thus equivalent to a death sentence:
"Of our sickness the most savage is to despise our being." It suffices to
consult on this subject the entire history of philosophy, which may be
summarized—if one excepts scattered, isolated cases such as Mon-

taigne and Nietzsche precisely—as a suit brought victoriously and won justly against existence and its fragility. From Parmenides and Plato through Kierkegaard and Heidegger, everything has been said on the subject, in the clearest and most incisive manner, to the extent that one is sometimes tempted to take the philosophers to task in the manner of Shakespeare's Friar Laurence, who scolds Romeo for threatening to kill himself:

> What, rouse thee, man! thy Juliet is alive,
> For whose dear sake thou wast but lately dead:
> There art thou happy. Tybalt would kill thee,
> But thou slewest Tybalt: there art thou happy.
> The law that threat'ned death becomes thy friend
> And turns it to exile: there art thou happy.
> A pack of blessings light upon thy back;
> Happiness courts thee in her best array;
> But, like a misbehav'd and sullen wench,
> Thou [pout'st upon] thy fortune and thy love.

> (3.3)

It follows from this incompatibility between joy and its rational justification—incompatibility which defines the paradox of joy—that joy, if it indeed exists, consists of an unthinkable rejoicing, a rejoicing which it is possible to feel but of which it is impossible to conceive in the absence of any possibility to explain it or to cover it with the mantle of authority of any argument whatsoever. But is it legitimate to deduce from the fact that joy is unthinkable the next conclusion which is often drawn in the same stroke of the pen, namely, that joy consists of an illusory rejoicing? I do not dare refer here to Kant's philosophy, which showed, or rather attempted to show, that the destiny of an "idea," even if it was revealed as inconceivable, was not necessarily doomed to the domain of the illusory. The examples he invokes to support his thesis—the immortality of the soul, freedom, the existence of God—remain entirely removed from my subject. But I would willingly accept from this Kantian reasoning process, put to work in the *Critique of Pure Reason* and the *Critique of Practical Reason,* the benefit of a supplementary clause in favor of joy, inviting the reader to recognize it as an experience that is simultaneously inconceivable and nonillusory. The alternative is simple and decisive, and I would add that it constitutes for me, until such time as I am more amply informed, the most serious question philosophy has ever had to treat. Either joy consists of an ephemeral illusion of having gotten rid of the tragic nature of existence, in which case joy is not paradoxical but illusory, or it consists of an approbation of existence which is held to be irremediably tragic, in which case joy is paradoxical, but it is not illusory.

It will come as no surprise to hear that I give my preference to the second alternative, persuaded as I am not only that joy succeeds in accommodating itself to the tragic but, in addition and especially, that it exists only in and by this paradoxical agreement with the tragic. It is precisely the privilege of joy and the reason for the particular contentment it gives—a contentment which is unique because it is the only one without reserve—to remain simultaneously conscious of and perfectly indifferent to the misfortunes of which existence is composed. This indifference to misfortune, concerning which I shall have more to say, does not mean that joy is inattentive to it, even less that it claims to ignore misfortune. On the contrary, it is eminently attentive to such calamity, the first affected and concerned by it, precisely because of the power of approbation, which permits joy to know it more and better than anyone. This is why I would say, to summarize briefly, that there is no true joy unless it is simultaneously thwarted, in contradiction with itself. Joy is paradoxical, or it is not joy.

The paradoxical character of joy has three principal consequences.

First consequence: joy is, by its very definition, of an illogical and irrational essence. It will always lack a convincing or even simply an avowable or expressible reason for being which would make it serious or coherent. Everyday language has much more to say on the subject that is generally thought when it speaks of "wild rejoicing" [*joie folle*] or says of someone that he is "beside himself with joy" [*fou de joie*]. Such expressions are not simply images. They must also be understood literally, for they express the truth itself: there is no joy which is not completely mad [*folle*]. Every joyful person is necessarily and in his or her own way a raving maniac.

Second consequence: joy is necessarily cruel, by virtue of the carefree attitude it exudes when faced with the most fatal destiny as well as the most tragic considerations. Not only is joy not a psychological affair, which would affect the ego and imply a feeling of personal happiness, but furthermore it appears to be indifferent to all feeling, provoking a sort of general insensitivity somewhat comparable to the "anesthesia of the heart" of which Bergson speaks in the context of laughter. The insouciance of joy, nevertheless, is not completely naive, or rather, it is so only in the second degree and as a last resort, that is, once everything is known and has been felt. This is something like the "second naïveté" which a modern interpreter of Mozart (Edwin Fisher) attributes quite correctly to Mozart in the last years of his life. There is no lack of corroboration for this quasi-primordial alliance between joy and cruelty, for the corrosive and implacable quality that belongs to all profound gaiety (as can be observed, for example, in the Spanish temperament). [E. M.] Cioran remarks in passing in *La Chute dans le temps* that "cruelty, in literature at least, is the sign of being among the chosen."[9] I would add for my part that cruelty is in every case a mark of distinction, and this is true in all domains—provided, of course, we understand cruelty not as pleasure taken in cultivating suffering but as a refusal of complacency toward any object, whatever it may be.

Third and last consequence: joy is the necessary condition, if not of life in general at least of life lived consciously and with full awareness. It consists of a madness which paradoxically permits one—and only it can grant such permission—to avoid all other madness, which preserves one from neurotic existence and permanent untruth. For this reason it constitutes the great and unique rule of the "art of living." True, there is nothing more difficult nor more arduous, nothing which seems more compromised from the very beginning, than such a knowledge or art. Montaigne's diagnosis of this case is well known. It comes at the end of the *Essays:* "There is nothing so beautiful and legitimate as to play the man well and properly, no knowledge so hard to acquire as the knowledge of how to live this life well and naturally. . . ."[10] The simple fact of taking reality into consideration, the simple exercise of reflection suffices here to discourage all effort—unless joy somehow comes to one's assistance, a joy which, like that of the Pascalian God, steps in when all forces are failing and brings about, *in extremis* and against all odds, the triumph of the weakest cause. This act of sustaining is defined by Pascal in the final apology of the second of the *Provincial Letters* precisely as an "extraordinary intervention." It remains to be said that the intervention of joy is forever mysterious, impenetrable even for those who feel its beneficent effects. In the final analysis, nothing has changed for them, and they understand no more than before. They have no new argument to invoke in favor of existence; they are still perfectly incapable of saying why or for what they are living; and yet from this moment forth they value life as indisputably and eternally desirable. This is the mystery inherent in the zest for life summarized by one of Hesiod's verses from the beginning of *Works and Days:* "Krupsantès gar ékousi théoi bion anthropoisi," (the gods ✗ have hidden what keeps men alive).

I would say, then, that the bolstering effect brought about by joy is necessary for life conceived as a knowledge of reality. There is, however, another way of accommodating reality, albeit a neurotic one, as I just suggested: it consists in denying reality or, more exactly, in considering its unhappy components not as inevitable but as provisional and capable of being eliminated progressively. It is evident that nothing is more frequent nor more modern than this sort of adapting to the real. This very day, for example, opening by chance a utilitarian weekly magazine, I read the following: "Coline Serreau believes that one can 'change the real.' A little courage, friendship, and shared confidence would suffice." I quote this fairly trivial reflection because it is representative of a manner of thinking that one can find just about anywhere, although in very different forms and expressed at times in less caricatural and more philosophical terms. This type of discourse, signed in this instance by a columnist for a television magazine, could have been read yesterday and can be read tomorrow in one's favorite publication but also in a respected work by such-and-such a celebrated thinker or philosopher. It should be remarked, nonetheless, that the spiritual sensitivity which it illustrates, if it is not recent, is not eternal either, nor is it inherent in human nature. Rather, it would seem characteristic of a certain mentality that is typically modern, of which it constitutes, to my mind, the most generic stylistic figure, what I would call its most common neuroticism. I find no trace of it, however, before the eighteenth century, probably because the turning away from reality, fundamentally assumed since the Enlightenment by the idea of progress, was accomplished before then by other forms of superstition and illusion.

To affirm the neurotic character of hope can, of course, seem paradoxical, since hope is generally held to be a virtue, that is, a force. There is no force more suspect than hope, however. It is doubtless not by chance nor due to a scribal error that Hesiod assimilates hope to the worst of all evils in *Works and Days,* to the plague that lies in Pandora's box, to the free disposition of men who rush into it with the idea that they will find there some salvation and the antidote to all other evils, when in fact it is simply one poison among others, if not poison par excellence. Everything which resembles hope or expectation constitutes, in fact, a vice, either a lack of force, a failing, or a weakness—a sign that living is no longer a given and finds itself attacked or compromised. It is a sign that the taste for life is lacking and that the pursuit of life must henceforth rely on a surrogate force, no longer on the taste for living the life that one is living but on the attraction of another and better life that no one will ever live. The man with hope is a man at the end of his resources and arguments, an empty man, literally exhausted, like the one of whom Schopenhauer speaks in a passage in *Parerga and Paralipomena,* who "hopes to find in medicinal broths and pharmaceutical drugs the health and the vigor of which the true source is the vital force itself."[11] On the contrary, joy constitutes force par excellence, true force, if only to the extent that it exempts one precisely from hope—an overwhelming force [*force majeure*] in comparison to which all hope appears to be laughable, a substitute, equivalent to a surrogate or to a replacement product.

That is why one should reply as follows to those who reproach the attitude of unconditional approbation of life (of which joy consists) for immediately approving of all human outrages and cruelties: this argument is invariably put forward by those specifically who lack the force to live and who hope confusedly that by reducing the scandals and horrors perpetrated by humanity—an honorable and justifiable task—they will also get rid of the misfortune inherent in existence, a neurotic thought. There is scarcely a desire to live better, especially if that desire dominates all other attention paid to existence, that is not the direct or thinly veiled expression of the simple incapacity to live which is the essence of mental derangement. All "progress"—or, rather, all progressivist ideology, by which I mean all excessive attention and suspicious enthusiasm for what has been or could be im-

proved in the human condition—in fact and inevitably implies the
mad project of a resolution of essential disorders by the reduction or
suppression of accidental disorders. As if a scientific discovery or a
better social organization would suffice to remove human beings from
their insignificant and ephemeral nature. It would be just as silly to say
that an improvement in street lighting would suffice to triumph over
cancer and death. Bypassing the essential, which one cannot change, in
favor of the nonessential, upon which one can act, doubtless authorizes a compensatory or hallucinatory satisfaction. But it is also, I
would reiterate in closing, the sign of a fundamental aberration, of a
confusion clearly pathological in character, even if it is typical of people whom no one would consider treating. That they should not be
treated is correct and doubly justified, moreover, for this kind of madness is generally without cure and without real importance, although it
is true that it can, under certain circumstances, provoke serious consequences for others—as is demonstrated by the political success of
certain collectivist ideologies.

= 2 =

Notes on Nietzsche

Preface

It has been said of the United States, not without malice nor doubtless a certain injustice, that it is one of the rare nations in the world to have evolved directly from barbarity to decadence without having gone through the stage of civilization. As much could be said of all great authors: they pass directly from being unknown by the public to being debased celebrities without ever experiencing the intermediate stage during which they would be simultaneously recognized and not betrayed. It is in fact impossible to avoid this forced shortcut, since notoriety signifies accession to the public domain and to insults of all sorts that are its necessary result. Thus, between obscurity and notoriety there will never be room for that chimerical ideal indicated by the expression to have a "good name" [*bon renom*]. [Maurice] Blanchot indeed wrote: "No, there will never be a way out for the dead, those who die after having written, and I never discerned in the most glorious posterity anything but a pretentious hell where the critics—all of us—play the roles of poor fools."[1] And reading certain pages that Blanchot himself devoted to Nietzsche,[2] one is grateful to him for the lucidity with which he places himself among the group of importunate critics—not that these pages are without pertinence, but because their pertinence belongs to a Hegelian preoccupation and allegiance. A praiseworthy lucidity in general, but ineffective in Nietzschean territory, like Heidegger's lucidity as he correctly thrashes the majority of Nietzsche's interpreters, but this time without any attention given to his own gesture, which, rather ironically, is itself implicated: "It is not the thinkers, but their interpreters, always better informed about them than they were about themselves, who in reality do not know what to say and thus pathetically dissimulate their perplexity by means of their incorrigible pendantry."[3]

As far as Nietzsche is concerned, I personally would distinguish two fundamental types of posthumous betrayal. From the end of the nineteenth century to the present, there have been two ways, *grosso modo,* of slighting Nietzsche (I am ignoring for the moment certain ways of "knowing" him, such as Heidegger's, to which I shall return and which demonstrate to my mind a much more pernicious failure to understand than any other form of ignorance). The first, which is now a little dated, consists in recognizing that Nietzsche thought and wrote *something,* but something bad, false, incoherent, immoral, and dangerous. The second, more recent, consists in maintaining that Nietzsche in some way thought or wrote *nothing,* but that, paradoxically, the essence of his force and finesse resides in this lacuna, as well as the reason for his present influence. This is a curious judgment, but it is certified and persistent, and it makes me think of the opinions of Mlle Anaïs on the subject of literature and modern art in Marcel Aymé's *Confort intellectuel:* "Her preference in literature went to Picasso and in painting to Jean Paulhan, who, not being a painter, was one nevertheless and all the more so."[4] In the same way, Nietzsche is readily extolled today as someone who, not being a philosopher, is one "nevertheless and all the more so": a great interpreter precisely because he interprets nothing, as Foucault put it during the Royaumont colloquium on Nietzsche, a great thinker exactly because he failed to think anything, as [Pierre] Klossowski has repeated on diverse occasions. A comparable asepticization of Nietzsche's remarks is manifest as well in the texts that Bataille, Blanchot, and Derrida have devoted to him. These are all commentaries which, if they do not purely and simply cancel out the fact of a Nietzschean thought (albeit for laudatory purposes), nevertheless obliterate the originality and importance of Nietzsche's contribution by assimilating it to what preoccupies them most, that is, respectively, the theology of eroticism, the modern destiny of Hegelianism, the sempiternal stealing away (or *différance*) of the truth. This assimilation is natural and legitimate up to a certain point, if only there were not an unfortunate circumstance in this case, namely, the fact that the preoccupations at stake are each time completely foreign to what interests Nietzsche. Furthermore, they directly contradict him and thus become targets of the very Nietzschean critical activity they pretend to illustrate. There are pre-Nietzschean interests which curiously reappear a century after Nietzsche, supposedly in his interest.

This modern method of ignoring Nietzsche by means of a commentary which is enthusiastic about the fact that Nietzsche does not think, or that he thinks along the lines of a post-Hegelian modernity, is equivalent to an outright rejection analogous to the one accomplished earlier by those who credited Nietzsche with a positive philosophy that was nonetheless faulty. It is a barely subtle variation. One should certainly explore the causes of such a rejection, which persists nearly a century after the death of Nietzsche. Its fundamental reason seems to me to reside in the fact that all totally affirmative discourses, such as Nietzsche's or that of Lucretius or Spinoza, are and always have been received as completely inadmissible. They are inadmissible not only in the eyes of the majority, as Bataille insinuated in his book on Nietzsche,⁵ but also—and I would add more particularly—in the eyes of the small group of those people called intellectuals. It is psychology's job, or perhaps that of psychopathology, to explain the mysterious link which so often unites the exercise of thought with the experience of pain, that strange "coincidence of thought and suffering" to which Klossowski refers in his own book on Nietzsche.⁶ Such a spiritual disposition is in any case completely rebellious to a philosophy in the Nietzschean style because it is prepared to undergo every ordeal except that of insouciance.

The fact remains that all of philosophical and literary modernity in France marches to the beat of Nietzsche's name and that nothing is more foreign to that modernity than Nietzschean thought. Or, more exactly, what is modern in Nietzsche resides not in Nietzsche at all but rather in the manner—quite "modern" because it is symptomatic of modern times—in which he is praised as something other than himself. If, on the one hand, there is little relation between Nietzschean thought and its modern commentators, on the other hand, the idea that the greatness of Nietzsche comes precisely from the fact that he is not a great thinker can appear as something very characteristic of our modernity. Doubtless Mlle Anaïs's formula quoted earlier is open to ridicule, but I believe one would be wrong to take it as an example of nothing but a snobbish foible of limited and already antiquated interest. The formula is more pertinent and penetrating than it seems, for all of our modernity subscribes to it profoundly—from Bataille to Lacan. To say that presence is forever absent or deferred, that the object of desire is to be sought not in itself but rather in everything that it is not, that in a general manner reality is not where one would believe but always elsewhere is ultimately to repeat in the intellectual mode what Mlle Anaïs expressed in a slightly simplistic manner when she said that Jean Paulhan was all the more a painter in that he did not paint. It is only from this farcical perspective that Nietzsche is taken seriously today and considered to be modern—as a witness of the other and a figure of the void.

1. Beatitude and Suffering

The man who has much joy must be a good man. But perhaps he is not the most intelligent one, even though he attains that to which the most intelligent men aspire with all of their intelligence.

—The Traveler and His Shadow

I shall borrow the term "beatitude" from the paper given by Henri Birault at the Royaumont colloquium on Nietzsche held in 1964, and I shall use it to define the central theme of Nietzschean philosophy.[7] Other terms would probably work just as well: joie de vivre, gladness, jubilation, pleasure of existence, adhesion to reality, and still others. The word is not important; what counts here is the idea or intention of an unconditional allegiance to the simple and unadorned experience of the real. Nietzsche's philosophical thought may be summarized and set apart by this. So let's use "beatitude," *Seligkeit,* to which we shall agree to give the honor of representing such a philosophy, to be, in essence, its duly accredited ambassador. It is doubtless no longer necessary today, as was required fifteen years ago,[8] to show how the theme of beatitude corresponds to the concepts recognized as fundamentally Nietzschean, at least as the "tradition" would have it: the superman, the eternal return, the will to power. The commentator of Nietzsche would now have to work at a task which is the inverse, showing on the contrary how these concepts correspond to the theme of beatitude, how they are its more or less direct expressions and variations. If and only if a concept is answerable to an absolute beatitude can it be recognized as specifically Nietzschean. The themes of the superman, the eternal return, the will to power (we have long known that if they are at the center of anything, they are at the center of a book which does not exist since it was never written) make sense only to the extent that they constitute tardy and haphazard expressions of beatitude, the central and constant theme of Nietzsche's thought—I would willingly say the *only* theme.

The first three aphorisms from book four of *The Gay Science*—a book subtitled *Sanctus Januarius,* "Saint January," and written during a euphoric winter in Genoa—will permit us to obtain a rather precise and complete idea of what beatitude is for Nietzsche.

The first of these texts, aphorism 276, entitled "For the new year," is presented in the form of a New Year's greeting containing intellectual instructions valid for all the years to come and for all that its author, who is also its addressee, will think in the future. This New Year's greeting which Nietzsche creates for himself consists of a general intention to be henceforth in agreement with all that exists, to live as an unconditional lover of reality considered under the auspices of a necessity that is so evident as to be no longer in need of foundation, of any type of "well-foundedness": "I want to learn more and more to see as beautiful what is necessary in things; then I shall be one of those who make things beautiful. *Amor fati:* let that be my love henceforth! I do not want to wage war against what is ugly. I do not want to accuse; I do not even want to accuse those who accuse. *Looking away* shall be my only negation. And all in all and on the whole: some day I wish to be only a Yes-sayer."[9]

The second text, aphorism 277, entitled "Personal providence," consists of what one might call the radicalization of the optimistic theses of Leibniz. In it the world appears not only as the best for all possible worlds when considered in general, but still more as the best of all possible worlds when considered in particular, even if considered solely in each of its instants, be it the worst, or in each of the creatures which compose it, be it the least favored by what Nietzsche would call fate and Leibniz the economy of good implied by universal harmony:

> For it is only now that the idea of a personal providence confronts us with the most penetrating force, and the best advocate, the evidence of our eyes, speaks for it—now that we can see how palpably always everything that happens to us turns out for the best. Every day and every hour, life seems to have no other wish than to prove this proposition again and again. Whatever it is, bad weather or good, the loss of a friend, sickness, slander, the failure of some letter to arrive, the spraining of an ankle, a glance into a shop, a counter-argument, the opening of a book, a dream, a fraud—either immediately or very soon after it proves to be something that "must not be missing"; it has a profound significance and use precisely for *us*. (223–24)

What appears here as a Nietzschean generalization of Leibnizian optimism naturally does not stand without an ultimate disavowal of Leibniz. While Leibniz attributes the organization of general providence to God, Nietzsche attributes the merit of this personal providence which watches over the fortune of each of us in particular to "chance" [*hasard*], conceived as an a-theistic principle, or rather as an antiprinciple:

> Well, I think that in spite of all this we should leave the gods in peace as well as the genii who are ready to serve us, and rest content with the supposition that our own practical and theoretical skill in interpreting and arranging events has now reached its high point. Nor should we conceive too high an opinion of this dexterity of our wisdom when at times we are excessively surprised by the wonderful harmony created by the playing of our instrument—a harmony that sounds too good for us to dare to give the credit to ourselves. Indeed, now and then someone plays with us—good old chance; now and then chance guides our hand, and the wisest providence could not think up a more beautiful music than that which our foolish hand produces then. (224)

It would be a misinterpretation to read in these lines the expression of an ultimate disenchantment, of a disillusion in the "moral" sense of

the term, because in this text by Nietzsche there is indeed a desire for
disillusion, but in the intellectual sense, that is, to remove an illusion
which is superfluous and foreign to true Nietzschean felicity. It would
seem as if the idea of a personal providence *added* to the experience of
beatitude, when in fact, in Nietzsche's eyes, it risks destroying it entirely. And this is so, may I reiterate, not because of some alleged
vanity on Nietzsche's part whose effect would be to disrupt the experience of felicity as soon as one has to thank some god for it. No thinker
pays more homage to existence or feels more obliged to speak of its
grace and justice than Nietzsche. Nietzsche does not pay homage
to God for existence because he believes, right or wrong, that the
concept of God is not a sufficiently *grateful* concept, a half-grateful
way of thinking which needs a divine guarantee to make up for the
multiple disadvantages or "deficiencies" attached to existence. Here
Nietzsche is squarely opposed to Leibniz, but only because he is, in a
manner of speaking, ultra-Leibnizian, a strange and incorrigible "ul-
tra" of optimism who believes, in short, that if Leibniz needed God, it
was only because he was not optimistic enough, that he did not believe
in bliss fully enough. Generally, moreover, Nietzsche links skepticism
not to disappointment but to a superabundance of bliss. And it goes
without saying that this is why his skepticism is without model and
without precursor in the history of philosophy, and notably in the
history of skeptical philosophy. Thus one finds this remarkable aphorism on the subject of Carlyle in *Twilight of the Idols,* to which I shall
return later: "The craving for a strong faith is no proof of a strong
faith, but quite the contrary. If one has such a faith, then one can
afford the beautiful luxury of skepticism: one is sure enough, firm
enough, has ties enough for that."[10]

The third text in this series which opens book 4 of *The Gay Science,*
aphorism 278, is entitled "The thought of death" and develops, on a
subject already thoroughly explored, an apparently hackneyed theme:
although the thought of our imminent disappearance permeates human life completely and at every instant, crying out our death without
relief, we perpetually take exception to this menacing presence, thinking and acting just as if death did not exist. Nothing is inspired here,
however, by well-known reflections concerning the specifically human
weakness which consists in putting the thought of death in parentheses

or in "repressing" it, in the psychoanalytic sense of the term, nor by the famous Pascalian analyses concerning amusement [*divertissement*] ("Men, being unable to ignore death, misery, and ignorance, decided, in order to remain happy, not to think about them"). The conclusion of the aphorism, and its very reason for being, go in exactly the opposite direction, since Nietzsche *credits* human conscience for its negligence in the face of death: "How strange it is that this sole certainty and common element makes almost no impression on people, and that nothing is further from their minds than the feeling that they form a brotherhood of death. It makes me happy that men do not want at all to think the thought of death! I should like very much to do something that would make the thought of life even a hundred times more appealing to them" (225). There is a complete reversal of perspective here with respect to traditional philosophy. According to the latter, the thought of death is such that it devalues definitively the thought of life, and, given this, it is in the individual's interest to live without thinking about it at all. According to Nietzsche, however, the thought of life is such that it renders the thought of death inoffensive, *and one reaches this decision in full lucidity.*

The neutralization of the thought of death—which is an augur of Freud's analyses revealing the triumphant power of humor, but at a higher level because it is more general—already partially belongs to what I would term the second register of Nietzschean thought: an essential register because it borders immediately on the first, indissociable from the theme of beatitude. The latter, in fact, always implies for Nietzsche the recognition and acceptance of all thoughts, including and especially those which are apparently the most opposed to him. Recognition, acceptance, or, still more precisely, *ingestion*. It is well known that Nietzsche often reasons in terms of rumination and ruminants. The idea of digestion occupied him so materially that he was even careful in *Ecce Homo* to give us long explanations of the diet that he had arranged for himself during his life, a diet to which he attributes a large part of the quality of his life and work. There are two species of ruminants for Nietzsche, however: those who ruminate ceaselessly but without succeeding in digesting (the case of the man of resentment) and those who ruminate and digest (the case of the Dionysian man)—good and bad ruminants. Generally the interpretation is as follows: the bad ruminant does not have access to bliss because he is the prisoner of a thought devoted to misfortune; the good ruminant accedes to bliss because he has surmounted the thought of misfortune and succeeds in digesting it. This is not, however, quite what Nietzsche thinks when it comes to rumination. If one looks at things, carefully, the distribution of roles is rather different. The good ruminant has access simultaneously *to bliss and to misfortune,* and the destiny of the bad ruminant is to have access to neither to one nor to the other. He does not know bliss since he does not succeed in digesting misfortune, but neither does he know misfortune, precisely because he does not succeed in digesting the thought of it. The man of bliss has access to everything, and notably to the knowledge of misfortune, while the man of misfortune has access to nothing, not even to the knowledge of his own misfortune. Since the thought of life includes the thought of death, so also and in the same manner the thought of bliss—beatitude—implies a profound and incomparable knowledge of misfortune. What I am calling here the second register of Nietzschean thought, witness and faithful companion of the first, consists of this knowledge.

This second register of Nietzschean thought—that is, the complete dossier of misfortune past, present, and future—concerns what Nietzsche all his life, from *The Birth of Tragedy* on, designated by the name "tragic" and associated with the "Dionysian," the first being the necessary condition of the second. There is no joy that has not been tested [*éprouvée*]—I mean, naturally, proven [*prouvée*], evidenced—by the knowledge of pain. This association of ideas is at the heart of everything Nietzsche feels and thinks; it is the foundation of his philosophy. This is a foundation which could take as its motto the formula of the poet Furius Antias, which Nietzsche quotes in the foreword to *Twilight of the Idols:* "Incresunt animi, virescit volnere virtus" (the wound stimulates and gives courage). Unless one would prefer the eighth aphorism of "Maxims and Arrows," which serve as an introduction to the same collection: "*Out of life's school of war:* What does not destroy me, makes me stronger" (*Twilight,* 465). Strictly speaking, almost all of Nietzsche's work could be invoked as an illustration of this secret alliance—sealed by Nietzsche at the time of *The Birth of Tragedy*—between misfortune and bliss, the tragic and the jubilatory, the experience of pain and the affirmation of joy. I shall simply cite here as a reminder several aphorisms taken from *Beyond Good and Evil*. Aphorism 212: "A philosopher—if today there could be philosophers—would be compelled to find the greatness of man, the concept of 'greatness,' precisely in his range and multiplicity, in his wholeness in manifoldness. He would even determine value and rank in accordance with how much and how many things one could bear and take upon himself, how *far* one could extend his reponsibility."[11] Aphorism 225: "The discipline of suffering, of *great* suffering—do you know that only *this* discipline has created all enhancements of man so far? That tension of the soul in unhappiness which cultivates its strength, its shudders face to face with great ruin, its inventiveness and courage in enduring, persevering, interpreting, and exploiting suffering, and whatever has been granted to it of profundity, secret, mask, spirit, cunning, greatness—was it not granted to it through suffering, through the discipline of great suffering?" (154). Aphorism 270: "One can almost classify human beings according to how profoundly they suffer" (220 [translation modified]). To these one must add, if one desires to be complete even in the most summary fashion, a formula from *Ecce Homo* found in the third aphorism of its foreword: "How much truth does a spirit *endure,* how much truth does it *dare?* More and more that became for me the real measure of value."[12] There is, in addition, the seventh aphorism of the 1886 preface to *The Traveler and His Shadow,* which makes of the "will to the tragic and to pessimism" the only guarantee against "the fearful and questionable that characterizes all existence,"[13] and, finally, the aphorism from *Twilight of the Idols* quoted earlier on the original manner in which Nietzsche conceives of the relation between skepticism and faith.

To finish, let me summarize the conclusions one may already draw for the present from this rapid reading of several of Nietzsche's aphorisms. Concerning beatitude, we can say that it is for Nietzsche the fundamental idea around which other ideas are organized and ordered. We also know that it consists of a pure and unconditional adherence to the real, which does not need the idea of providence, nor, of course, a philosophy of history, but implies, by contrast, a knowledge of the tragic. As for knowledge of the tragic, we know that it is not considered by Nietzsche to be a mutilation of joy, a portion subtracted from beatitude by the effect of suffering, but that it constitutes, on the contrary, an additional gaiety which wins out over suffering just as the idea of life triumphs over the idea of death. It is thus presented as a test of beatitude, a "trial" [*épreuve*] in the double sense of the term, put to the test and proven, in other words, a *crucial experiment* in the way Bacon understood it. In a reciprocal and complementary argument, Nietzsche repeats incessantly that every thought which is not penetrated by a knowledge of the tragic, which attempts to evade the evidence of death, of the ephemeral, of suffering inevitably produces philosophical cures, such as Eleatic ontology or Platonic metaphysics, invoked less to account for existence than to call it into question untiringly.

2. Nietzsche and Music

> Having "wax in one's ears" was then almost a
> condition of philosophizing; a real philosopher
> no longer listened to life insofar as life is music;
> he *denied* the music of life—it is an ancient
> philosopher's superstition that all music is
> sirens' music.
>
> —*The Gay Science*

The fundamental problem of Nietzsche's philosophy is presented apparently as a Kantian problem: Is Nietzschean beatitude—that is, the pure adhesion to existence without remorse or afterthought—possible? How is the transformation of suffering into a positive experience of affirmation possible? How is it that the thought of death has no effect on the thought of life other than a favorable one? One is obviously free to elude these questions by responding simply that this is surely possible since it is the case. And this is assuredly what Nietzsche would be authorized to respond, since all of his work is precisely the narrative and the testimony of such a beatitude. It should be remarked, however, that the fact of an affirmation without a shadow of negativity is based on no avowed reasoning, cannot appeal to any thought on which to stand and in which to find the outline of a foundation—even if one delves deeply into the thoughts of Nietzsche himself. Nietzsche analyzes ideas that are foreign to him in light of his experience of beatitude, but there is no critical analysis with respect to his own beatitude, which is doubtless affirmed but never analyzed or criticized, in fact almost never described, except by vague or fleeting allusions or incidents. The fulcrum on which the system rests is thus simultaneously highly operative and almost invisible, like a site from which a summons emanates for every destination, while that very site itself remains outside the purview of its own invocation.

This fundamental question of Nietzschean thought, however, differs from Kantian interrogations in that it receives a positive response from lived and immediate experience (while the great questions of Kant are answered only by the intercession of a metaphysical distinction between the empirical and the "transcendental," the phenomenon and the "noumenon"). More credible thus than the possibility of the synthetic a priori judgment or of the fundamental regulatory ideas of morals, whose destiny depends on the credit accorded or not to another world, the possibility of Nietzschean beatitude is already guaranteed in the here and now—by the readily repeatable experience of *musical* jubilation. Music is what occupies all the "nerve centers" of Nietzsche's philosophy, where it replaces precisely everything which serves as a principle or foundation in other systems. It is what answers all the questions and thus takes the place simultaneously of theology, metaphysics, and physics. It is the first Revelation which teaches once and for all and sufficiently what there is to know about the meaning, cause, and end of all existence. If Nietzsche refuses metaphysics and religion, it is precisely because they would occupy a space already inhabited by music in his thought. Since the majority of modern commentators on Nietzsche share the common trait of ignoring the question of music, it is doubtless necessary to remind oneself here of the primordial and constitutive importance of music in the genesis of Nietzschean thought. Nietzsche wrote and repeated: "Without music, life would be an error" (*Twilight,* 471). Weighty words on the part of a thinker whose whole philosophy can be summarized as a perpetual admiration of life. It is easy to deduce from this that without music there would be no Nietzschean philosophy. In fact Nietzsche is not simply a philosopher-musician, as everyone necessarily agrees. He is first of all and especially a musician-philosopher, a musician led to philosophical meditation by an unceasing reflection on the nature of musical jubilation. The shared essence of the "tragic" and the "Dionysian," which constitutes the thread of all Nietzsche's philosophy beginning with *The Birth of Tragedy* and including the rectifications which its author himself accomplished following its publication, is already designated by the title of Nietzsche's first work as an effect of music, that is, as a consequence of music, provided one is careful to read this title all the way to the end: *The Birth of Tragedy from the Spirit of Music.* This elementary remark on the importance of music for Nietzsche can take on the value of an opinion, posthumous or antedated, aimed at past or future interpreters of Nietzschean thought: "Let no man enter here who is not a geometer." Such was, if one is to believe tradition, the motto of Plato, the purpose of which was to choose those who would enter his Academy. Different but just as rigorous could be Nietzsche's motto: Let no man be concerned with me unless he is a musician.

To summarize the essence of the relation between Nietzschean thought and music I would propose two complementary theses. First thesis: musical experience in Nietzsche always coincides with an experience of beatitude. Second thesis: reciprocally, the experience of beatitude, even when it is felt and described in the context of a nonmusical reality, is always for Nietzsche the secondary effect of jubilation which is first and foremost of a musical order. Thus, music is in every case at the origin of what Nietzsche experiences as beatitude. The origin of tragedy is the exemplary case, and Nietzsche's first book precisely and expressly situates it in music.

The first of these theses is hardly open to discussion. It is evident in itself, and we need only read Nietzsche to convince ourselves of its exactness. Not that music can never be nostalgic or melancholic, but Nietzsche turns his ear away from such music. Everything that Nietzsche wrote on the subject of music, his tastes and preferences in music, even the music composed by Nietzsche himself demonstrate an indissoluble alliance between musical experience as Nietzsche conceives of it and the experience of jubilation. A remark in *Ecce Homo* concerning the "case of Wagner" contains the essential, defining the musical effect as the power to say yes to the world (317). One of the musicians preferred by Nietzsche was Chopin: "I [would] . . . surrender the rest of music for Chopin," writes Nietzsche in *Ecce Homo* (251). Chopin, contrary to an opinion still in vogue today, is diametrically opposed to romanticism because he excels in the expression of *bliss*. Chopin is happy even in misfortune (just as Nietzsche's Dionysus lives in affirmation even in the tragic); even his melancholy is for him a supplementary occasion for delight—a delight often interpreted as morose and morbid, when, on the contrary, it is the sign of the greatest health. And his happiness is such, says aphorism 160 of *The Traveler and His Shadow,* that the most blessed among the gods, upon hearing Chopin's "Barcarole," would suddenly want to share the condition of men, even the most miserable of them (*Human, All Too Human*, 347). To sum up briefly Nietzsche's doctrine on this point, one can say that music constitutes in his eyes a triple apprenticeship, a triple initiation: initiation to bliss, initiation to life, initiation to philosophy. Initiation, of course and first of all, to bliss: "How little is required for pleasure! The sound of a bagpipe" (*Twilight*, 471). But also initiation to life and to philosophy. To life, as attested, for example, by the pages of "The Case of Wagner" devoted to *Carmen,* whose "sense of the real" Nietzsche celebrates above all, the manner in which Bizet's music succeeded in evoking the primitiveness belonging to everything which comes into existence, its *irrecusable* character, as quick and inevitable as the blade of a guillotine: "From Mérimée it still has the logic in passion, the shortest line, the *harsh* necessity; above all, it has what goes with the torrid zone: the dryness of the air, the *limpidezza* in the air. In every respect, the climate is changed. Another sensuality, another sensibility speaks here, another cheerfulness. This music is cheerful, but not in a French or German way. Its cheerfulness is African; fate hangs over it; its happiness is brief, sudden, without pardon."[14] And, finally, to philosophy, recognized in "The Case of Wagner" again and in the context of the discussion of *Carmen* as an effect itself blessed by the happiness provided by listening to music, that is, as a reflection brought forth by musical bliss and which would never have been thus "reflected" without the aid of music:

> How such a work makes one perfect! One becomes a "masterpiece" oneself. Really, every time I heard *Carmen* I seemed to myself more of a philosopher, a better philosopher, than I generally consider myself: so patient do I become, so happy, so Indian, so settled. . . . Has it been noticed that music liberates the spirit? gives wings to thought? that one becomes more of a philosopher the more one

becomes a musician?—The gray sky of abstraction rent as if by
lightning; the light strong enough for the filigree of things; the great
problems near enough to grasp; the world surveyed as from a
mountain.—I have just defined the pathos of philosophy. ("Wagner," 157–58)

The second thesis, according to which musical jubilation would be
for Nietzsche the principle of every experience of beatitude, the principle, then, of everything which Nietzsche recognizes to be of value and
consequently the keystone of Nietzschean philosophy, naturally appears more problematic. I shall attempt to show, nevertheless, first that
it is exact—in other words, it respects Nietzsche to the letter—and
next that it is in profound agreement with what is most remarkable in
Nietzschean thought—I mean the affirmation of an unconditional jubilation with regard to all reality whatever it may be, musical or nonmusical, "good" or "bad." For Nietzsche it suffices—and this is perhaps the last word on his philosophy—that a thing be real for it to be
immediately considered good, and vice versa (the domain of what is
bad, that is, suspicious for Nietzschean "morality," is constituted by
the set of things which do not exist, or more precisely by the set of
ideas which designate them in the eyes of men).

On the first point—the material exactness of the thesis—I will first
invoke in a general manner the fact that Nietzsche always granted a
primacy, of both a hierarchical and a chronological order, to song and
the musical score over any other form of text, whether spoken or
written. Prose, poetry, theater all have music as their model and origin.
That is the point upon which *The Birth of Tragedy* insists, notably in
the fifth and sixth aphorisms. The model of all discourse, musical
discourse is thus the model of the most elaborate form of discourse,
philosophical writing, at least as Nietzsche understands and practices
it. And he declares that he writes as much with his foot as with his
hand, with the foot which dances on paper and counts the measures
(*The Gay Science,* aphorism 52). I would further invoke, as a specific
illustration, a passage from *The Gay Science*—the beginning of aphorism 334, entitled "One must learn to love"—in which Nietzsche
makes of musical taste and of it long apprenticeship the mode of the
love for the real and of the learned "acclimatization" such a love
presupposes:

> This is what happens to us in music: First one has to *learn to hear* a
> figure and melody at all, to detect and distinguish it, to isolate it and
> delimit it as a separate life. Then it requires some exertion and good
> will to *tolerate* it in spite of its strangeness, to be patient with its
> appearance and expression, and kindhearted about its oddity. Fi-
> nally there comes a moment when we are *used* to it, when we wait
> for it, when we sense that we should miss it if it were missing; and
> now it continues to compel and enchant us relentlessly until we have
> become its humble and enraptured lovers who desire nothing better
> from the world than it and only it. But that is what happens to us
> not only in music. That is how we have *learned to love* all things
> that we now love. (262)

It remains to be shown how the thesis which makes music the condition *sine qua non* of all beatitude comes from the best Nietzschean
orthodoxy, that is, harmonizes with a thought characterized by a universal approbation of all reality. One clarification is necessary here. It
is certain that musical experience was always for Nietzsche the principal path leading toward the philosophical experience of approbation.
That does not at all mean, however, that Nietzschean approbation of
reality is limited to its specifically musical aspect, to the perspective on
the world offered by music—as if it were necessary to reject from the
real everything which is not transfigured by musical perspective.
Among all experiences musical jubilation is obviously privileged, not
because this jubilation privileges and distinguishes musical reality
among all other realities, but because it has as its effect, in Nietzsche's
opinion, to arouse the approbation of all things indifferently. Doubtless one finds an ambiguous declaration in the fifth aphorism of *The
Birth of Tragedy,* according to which existence and the world have no
justification other than the fact that they constitute, in the eyes of
whoever knows how to appreciate them, an aesthetic phenomenon.
Nietzsche came back to this formula in the 1886 preface to *The Birth
of Tragedy,* however, when he called his declaration a "scabrous proposition." One could also invoke in this context the aphorism from
Twilight of the Idols, quoted earlier, according to which "without
music, life would be an error." But it would be best not to lose sight of
the fact that in Nietzsche music functions as a witness to the world and
not at all as an alternative offered to the world in the form of a safe
haven. Such a formula thus simply means that life deprived of its own

approbation (music invites such approbation in a particularly imperious manner, at least for certain people, Nietzsche among them) would cease immediately to be life, not that life deprived of music would cease to be life. It is out of the question for Nietzsche to appeal to another world, even a musical one, to justify this world. What is of value in music is the fact that it is witness to this world, an expression all the more precious for being resolutely wedded to the here and now. The Nietzschean affirmation of the real indeed takes place through the experience of music, but it does not concern musical reality alone. It must be understood—and in fact is understood by those who have the ears to hear it—for every kind of existence. And that is why Nietzsche says, in aphorism 372 of *The Gay Science,* quoted earlier as an epigraph, that traditional philosophy, from Plato to Kant, was principally and permanently concerned with covering its ears. Not that it refused, as in the case of Ulysses, to allow itself to be charmed by the Sirens' song, which it treated like an evocation of a utopic world, of an illusory and deceitful reality. Quite the contrary. Traditional philosophy did not want to hear about the real, which is precisely what the Sirens' song evokes unceasingly.

3. Musical Gaiety

Given the central role that jubilation and the experience of music play, the former always linked to the latter in Nietzsche, the credibility of Nietzschean thought appears as a tributary to the credibility of a conception of music roughly but in certain ways already definitively outlined in *The Birth of Tragedy.* This is a conception that one can sum up in two complementary and reciprocal propositions. First proposition: music signifies gaiety; music is in its essence gay. Second proposition: inversely, gaiety presupposes music; gaiety is in its essence musical. It is out of the question to attempt to establish the universal validity of such propositions, to give them the force of a kind of certainty or truth. Exceptions manifestly abound to the point of undercutting the law: many sad spirits are infatuated by music; many gay spirits remain ignorant of it forever. That does not mean, however, that Nietzschean thought finds here a general ground for invalidation. It might just be, in fact—and this is actually the case—that its dominant theme, gaiety, concerns those who accede to joy without experiencing the mediation of musical gaiety, just as it contradictorily concerns those who experience the pleasure of music without thereby acceding to joy. To establish, in addition, the Nietzschean validity of these two propositions, which can be reputed neither true nor false, to demonstrate that such a complementary relationship between gaiety and music is true at least of Nietzsche, who affirms it himself explicitly in all of his work, would constitute a task every bit as vain. The only plausible question consists in asking whether these two propositions, which can be held to be neither true nor false, can be considered believable, that is, possessing a meaning sufficiently consistent to be held true by some and from a certain point of view.

I shall begin by an examination of the second proposition: that it is the essence of gaiety to be musical. My remarks will be short, however, because the proposition does not lend itself to useful discussion. In Nietzsche's work, as in that of others, music is the most intense moment of vital jubilation, a pleasure comparable to and superior to any other physical or psychic pleasure, notably sexual pleasure. It is just as evident, however, that the jubilatory sentiment of being, the pleasure of existing, is present in many independent of any musical interest. All that one can thus say is that for Nietzsche and certain others, the joy of being culminates in musical expression, where it finds its supreme and ultimate accomplishment. For others it is quite different, and there is naturally no reason to conclude that their jubilation is less strong.

I thus return without further discussion to an examination of the first proposition, namely, that it is of the essence of music to be gay. This is an apparently scabrous proposition because the opposite opinion is assuredly the most common one. Doubtless it is generally admitted that music can be gay, but only of an accidental gaiety, owing to an effect which is somehow accessory or supplementary to its real vocation, which would be to evoke melancholy and sadness in order to "sublimate" them. A remark made by Sergei Rachmaninoff—"music is the child of sorrow"—sums up an ancestral and perennial diagnosis. It would be useful to be precise about what this means: music is not sorrow but an effect of sorrow, a remedy for sorrow. In itself music is not at all sorrow but bliss, precisely to the extent that it is a remedy for sorrow—a negative and compensatory bliss, true, since it consists of a partial and momentary subtraction from the suffering attached to existence. In short, there is a give and take—a little more music, a little less reality. The time of music is thus assimilated to a time of retreat earned from the world, a "time to breathe" when one is faced with the urgency of the real. This conception of musical respite, of music as respite, is obviously the indication of a certain suffering with respect to the real. It is unmistakably the position of those who feel a sentiment of insufficiency and lack with regard to reality in general and their existence in particular. An important passage of *The Gay Science,* aphorism 370, entitled "What is romanticism?" defines this sentiment of lack as the essence of "romanticism" (that is, a profound tendency of the human spirit which escapes the boundaries of the historical period designated as Romantic), as opposed to the sentiment of plenitude which is characteristic of any "classical" artist. Naturally, music can be pressed into service to express this lack, as the work of illustrious and admirable composers abundantly illustrates. It does not follow, however, that such a music is eminently musical. If the eminence of music, the foremost point of its effect, resides in the approbation of the real, in a power to say yes to the world, then the musical expression of sadness (even if sadness is surmounted by the very benefit of music with a soothing and compensatory virtue) appears to be a sort of betrayal. It appears not as a properly musical expression but as a misuse of the musical effect for purposes other than the one to which music can eminently pretend, namely, the granting of a joy without reticence and without lack. Such a misuse of effect is present, for example, in the music of Schumann, of which Nietzsche said in aphorism 161 of *The Traveler and His Shadow* that its purpose was to evoke "the eternal youth" but that its result was to make one think of "the eternal old maid" (*Human, All Too Human,* 347). It is also present in the rupture which separates the art of Mozart from that of Beethoven, a rupture that is often interpreted as a passage from the less profound to the more profound, the accession of a superficial, light gaiety to a happiness that is purposeful and acquired with difficulty through suffering, a happiness consequently more solid and durable. Other interpreters with a more discerning ear judge this transition from Mozart to Beethoven inversely and diagnose in it a deterioration of joy, which, ceasing to be unconditional delight in order to become a reasoned happiness, moves from the more durable to the less durable and from the more profound to the less profound. According to them there is even in Beethoven, in addition to the misuse of the musical effect, a general turning of art against itself, as Roland Manuel suggests when he sees in Beethoven not a princely artist but the "prince of the rebels against art."[15] Perhaps one goes a little far in insulting Beethoven when one honors Mozart by evoking here a well-known passage from *Zarathustra:* "Life is a well of joy, but where the rabble drinks too, all wells are poisoned."[16] Nietzsche himself declares, however, in aphorism 245 of *Beyond Good and Evil:*

> The "good old time" is gone, in Mozart we hear its swan song. How fortunate we are that his rococo still speaks to us, that his "good company," his tender enthusiasms, his childlike delight in curlicues and Chinese touches, his courtesy of the heart, his longing for the graceful, those in love, those dancing, those easily moved to tears, his faith in the south, may still appeal to some *residue* in us. Alas, some day all this will be gone—but who may doubt that the understanding and taste for Beethoven will go long before that! Beethoven was after all merely the final chord of transition in style, a style break, and not, like Mozart, the last chord of a centuries-old great European taste. (180)

It is rather peculiar that gaiety, whether of musical order or not, must ceaselessly be defended against an insistent tendency of the human spirit to see in it nothing but a sentiment, agreeable certainly but of negligible importance on the whole, something that one could not really take seriously, when in fact it is perhaps the only thing in the world which could reasonably claim such an honor. Pure gaiety, which is veiled by absolutely no shadow of reserve, is easily suspected of frivolity, when it is actually the most profound of feelings, or accused of vulgarity, when it is actually the most noble of all sentiments. Cioran sums up the general reticence with regard to gaiety very well when he writes: "Everything which is exempt from a funereal tinge, even ever so slight, is necessarily vulgar."[17] For my part, I would oppose such a formula with its exact inverse: Everything which is not mixed with the funereal, not even with the slightest hint of it, is eminently noble. In the same vein, Roland Manuel makes this rather remarkable statement on the subject of Manuel de Falla's *Three-*

Cornered Hat: "Nothing is vulgar in Spain, not even gaiety" (*Manuel de Falla,* 44). The formula most certainly reveals a shared and common feeling with respect to gaiety, but it remains nonetheless rather surprising in its implications. The "not even" with which the author accompanies gaiety clearly suggests that the place of gaiety is ordinarily the place of vulgarity, in such a way that it is the extraordinary performance of Spain to succeed in being gay without falling into vulgarity. Reticence with respect to gaiety in general is naturally *a fortiori* valid with respect to musical gaiety. A music which is gay and nothing but gay is instinctively relegated by many to a "second order," to the domain of music which is at best anodyne and at worst vulgar. It does not bring to its listeners any affective energy worthy of interest or attention. Such a music, however, which is gay and nothing but gay is not in the least removed from the varied register of human emotions. Quite the contrary, it knows more about them than anyone, bringing them all together, even the worst of them, those that the most melancholic disposition never succeeds in representing perfectly, into the melting pot of its universal lightness. Is its very lightness not, moreover, the expression of the most moving of all emotions, namely, joy, considered precisely by Spinoza to be the first and principal affection to which human beings are subject?

There is a musician whose classicism Nietzsche could have opposed to Wagnerian romanticism just as welll as Bizet's, namely, Jacques Offenbach, considered light and superficial because he reduces musical effect to its simplest expression, of a sovereign and irresistible gaiety—a gaiety which is quite simply prodigious in the eyes of Offenbach, who is naively surprised himself: "But what did I do to God to deserve so much joy?" And considered vulgar—even the "king of musical vulgarity," if we are to believe a famous critic[18]—because his music contains the most intense emotion under the mask of parody and farce, like that of Mozart before him and Ravel after him. This opinion is all the more credible, moreover, in that Offenbach's musical distinction is very often eclipsed by the effective vulgarity of its interpretation. This confirms abundantly— whether it be a question of the singers, of the orchestra and its conductor, of the director, or of the libretto's or score's "arranger"— the well-founded nature of the penetrating judgment of another famous music critic: "There is no bad music, only music badly played."[19] This is a formula which is applied, naturally, to gifted musicians and to their supposedly minor or unsuccessful compositions. But this is not the place to bring musical and technical arguments against the widely held opinion which relegates Offenbach to the level of minor musicians, if not pseudomusicians, to speak of the originality and modernity of his rhythm, the Mozartian grace of his melody, the incomparable manner which he has of submitting the French language to a musical treatment against which it generally rebels so successfully. I will only recall a late and eloquent judgment by Nietzsche, who must have known Offenbach only through rather rare performances and who remarked in 1887: "The Jews have reached genius in the sphere of art with Heine and Offenbach."

4. Surface and Profundity

We have all read in the past few years, in remarks penned by numerous commentators on Nietzsche, that Nietzschean philosophy prefers surface to profundity, appearance to the real, the copy to the model, and, generally, the parody of reality to reality itself—even the parody of doctrine to the expression of any coherent doctrine, as Pierre Klossowski has maintained. The philosophy of Nietzsche would thus consist of a sort of sophistry destined to cover up the path of the truth and to make every contact with reality disappear from the minds of those who would undertake to follow that path. Such a thesis can certainly claim to have been accepted unanimously by the commentators, who have all recently taught it under one form or another. Set squarely against it, however, is the fact that it is in formal opposition to the general inspiration of Nietzschean thought, as well as to the totality of Nietzsche's texts dealing with the relations between surface and profundity. It is certain that Nietzsche always privileged surface, appearance, representation. But he did this less to the detriment of the profundity of the real than to the detriment of the illusory and false profundity attributed by traditional metaphysics to the notion of the "true world," which would be opposed to the reality of immediate experience, to the empirical reality of the senses. For Nietzsche, the surface is not what is opposed to profundity, but, on the contrary, that which permits profun-

● dity to be visible, that by which profundity manifests itself, as attested
by the Greeks of the classical period, of whom Nietzsche writes at the
beginning of *The Gay Science* that they were "superficial—*out of
profundity*" (38). It is thus impossible to deduce from the privilege
Nietzsche accords to appearance a type of philosophy which would
praise seeming in opposition to the real, the praise of appearance is of
one with the praise of the real because the space of representation is for
Nietzsche precisely the place where things are found, the very place-
ment, the exact site of the real.[20]

If Nietzsche wages war against every expression of a "veracity"
superior to what can be experienced here and now as true, it is because
these expressions are in his eyes just so many attacks perpetrated
against the real, a "curse on reality," as the foreword to *Ecce Homo*
states (218). It is impossible to quote here all the formulas in which
Nietzsche explicitly declares that his critique of the idea of a true
world situated above the world of appearances is always conducted *in
favor of reality,* not in favor of an appearance which would reveal
some supposed inconsistency of the world. I will nevertheless recall
certain of the most characteristic aphorisms. *The Gay Science,* aphorism 54: "What is 'appearance' for me now? Certainly not the opposite of some essence: what could I say about any essence except to
name the attributes of its appearance?" *Twilight of the Idols,* the
section entitled " 'Reason' in Philosophy," the second aphorism: "The
'apparent' world is the only one: the 'true' world is only added by a
lie" (481). *Ecce Homo,* preface, second aphorism: "The 'true world'
and the 'apparent world'—that means: the mendaciously invented
world and reality" (218). But there is more. Nietzsche takes care to
point out—and this is decisive—that the philosophy of appearance is
ultimately a vapor which dissipates as soon as that other vapor constituted by the idea of a "true world" itself dissipates: "*With the true
world we have also abolished the apparent one*" (*Twilight,* 486). The
nature and particularity of Nietzschean "ontology" is crystal clear
here: Nietzsche's conception of "being" is as opposed to Parmenides'
as it is to Heidegger's. It consists of the doctrine of a being which is
completely present in its own appearing. Surface and appearance are
in no way opposed to profundity and reality. On the contrary, for
Nietzsche they designate the very profundity of the real, that is, reality

in its appearance as "complete" since it lacks nothing, the real as unique and without a double.

In fact, in the sixth proposition aphorism of the section of *Twilight of the Idols* entitled " 'Reason' in Philosophy," Nietzsche summarizes in four simple theses his thought on the crucial point of the relation between the real and appearance, a thought which he qualifies precisely as "so essential and so new an insight." What follows is the complete text of the aphorism:

> *First proposition.* The reasons for which "this" world has been characterized as "apparent" are the very reasons which indicate its reality; any other kind of reality is absolutely undemonstrable.

> *Second proposition.* The criteria which have been bestowed on the "true being" of things are the criteria of not-being, of *naught;* the "true world" has been constructed out of contradiction to the actual world: indeed an apparent world, insofar as it is merely a moral-optical illusion.

> *Third proposition.* To invent fables about a world "other" than this one has no meaning at all, unless an instinct of slander, detraction, and suspicion against life has gained the upper hand in us: in that case, we avenge ourselves against life with a phantasmagoria of "another," a "better" life.

> *Fourth proposition.* Any distinction between a "true" and an "apparent" world—whether in the Christian manner or in the manner of Kant (in the end, an underhanded Christian)—is only a suggestion of decadence, a symptom of the *decline of life.* That the artist esteems appearance higher than reality is no objection to this proposition. For "appearance" in this case means reality *once more,* only by way of selection, reinforcement, and correction. The tragic is no pessimist: he is precisely the one who says Yes to everything questionable, even to the terrible—he is *Dionysian.* (484)

Such a text is in itself quite clear and explicit. It demonstrates abundantly that Nietzsche does not oppose appearance to reality but, on the contrary, unites them so that both oppose the illusion of a "true world." The sole difficulty resides evidently in the concept of appearance itself, which is used by Nietzsche in two different and opposite meanings: one whereby it qualifies or artistically "repeats" the real world and another whereby it designates, on the contrary, the "true world" as metaphysical thinking conceives of it. In its opposition to the supposed true world, the world of appearance—simply because it "appears"—constitutes the real world. Yet such a "true world" itself constitutes a purely "apparent" world, this time in the pejorative and illusory sense of the word: "an optical and moral illusion."

It is clear that the third section of *Twilight of the Idols*, entitled "How in the end the 'true world' became a fable," served as a pretext for Pierre Klossowski to suggest that in Nietzsche the order of truth was entirely dependent on the order of fabulation. Thus the truest world, the most real one, never constituted anything for Nietzsche but the uncertain subject of a story or myth: "The world became fable, the world as such is only fable. A fable signifies something which is told, an event which is told and thus an interpretation—religion, art, science, history, just so many different interpretations of the world, or rather, just so many variants of the fable."[21] Such an interpretation is admissible only through an enormous misprison which would consist—and in the case of Klossowski does indeed consist—in assimilating the diametrically opposite notions of "true world" and "truth." Even in Nietzsche—and this is after all a point in common with all other philosophers—the truth remains the opposite of falsehood. Consequently, if the "true world" is for Nietzsche a falsehood, this does not mean that the world in its appearance is a fable, rather, quite the contrary, that it is truthful and constitutes reality. Needless to say, the type of thinking according to which "the world as such is only a fable" would unfailingly be considered by Nietzsche as the sign of a devaluation of life and a vengeance directed against it.

Aphorism 54 of *The Gay Science*, quoted earlier, has the particularity of putting on the same level the question of surface and that of the mask, of suggesting that the relation of the surface to profundity is the same as that of the mask to the person wearing it: "What is 'appearance' for me now? Certainly not the opposite of some essence: what could I say about any essence except to name the attributes of its appearance? Certainly not a dead mask that one could place on an unknown x or remove from it!" (116). Just as the surface figures the visibility of what is below the surface, the mask figures the visibility of the "person" (moreover the Latin word *persona*, from which comes the French word *personne*, designates in the first place precisely the

theatrical mask). It is well known that all of Nietzsche's work demonstrates a constant interest in masks and disguises. The gift of the mask
is even described, in a passage often quoted from *Beyond Good and
Evil*, aphorism 278, as the most precious offering one can propose to
the lost voyager, perhaps because the mask is also what protects one
from shame—and the action which consists in protecting one from
shame is considered by Nietzsche the essence of the good action if one
is to believe aphorism 274 of *The Gay Science*: "*What do you consider
most humane?*—To spare someone shame" (220). The Nietzschean
status of the mask is nonetheless very particular. The mask never
appears in Nietzsche as a true disguise, an index of falsehood, and an
occasion to trick. Quite the contrary, it appears rather, and somewhat
curiously, as one of the best and surest indices of the real. It shares with
the real its profundity, its richness, and even its aristocratic nature, as
aphorism 40 of *Beyond Good and Evil* attests: "Whatever is profound
loves masks. . . . There are occurrences of such a delicate nature that
one does well to cover them up with some rudeness to conceal them;
there are actions of love and extravagant generosity after which nothing is more advisable than to take a stick and give any eyewitness a
sound thrashing: that would muddle his memory" (50). The mask also
shares the truth with the real, and that is what constitutes its nobility
in every case, even in the case of vulgar and meridional masquerade
evoked in aphorism 77 of *The Gay Science*, which profoundly defines
the noble as that which is absolutely at ease in existence (however
"vulgar" it may be in other ways), the non-noble as that which feels
even the slightest uneasiness or shame in existing (whatever may be its
"distinction"): "What is and remains popular is the *mask*. Hence there
is no point in objecting to the element of masquerade in the melodies
and cadenzas, in the leaps and jollities that mark the rhythms of these
operas. . . . What can we understand of that as long as we do not
understand the delight in masks and the good conscience in using any
kind of mask?" (132).[22]

In addition to the fundamental character of the mask—that is, to be
expression and not dissimulation—one can distinguish in Nietzsche
two principal functions for it. First function: one of modesty—it
serves to avoid exhibiting one's own richness of character everywhere
and to everyone. This is the principal meaning of several aphorisms on

the mask, notably the famous aphorism from *Beyond Good and Evil*
quoted earlier. There is, however, a second function of the Nietzschean
mask: it serves to express the eternal insufficiency of all words and of
every truth, even the most profound and most decisive, because they
are necessarily partial and affected by the point of view from which
they are enunciated. This is an insufficiency which results less from
any paucity on the mask's part than, on the contrary, from its own
excessive richness (here one can point out a convergence, distant at
best, between Nietzsche's thought and the Hegelian concept of the
"moment" when the truth of any thesis finds itself imprisoned). If
everything which is profound likes to mask itself, as aphorism 40 of
Beyond Good and Evil would have it, this is because the mask is the
mark of profundity and richness, and of a richness such that it could
never be contained in the space of a thought or of an aphorism—or of
a book. In addition to its ordinary task, which consists in saying what
it says, it thus remains for the Nietzschean aphorism to give homage to
all that it is not, to all that it necessarily leaves in the shadow—in the
way that the mask fulfills the duty of revelation not only of what it
signals directly but still more and especially of what it would have to
signal additionally. This consideration gives weight to Karl Schlechta's
thesis according to which a "second voice" can be heard in all Nietzschean texts, with the exception of the aphorisms left aside by Nietzsche and published posthumously, especially in the group of aphorisms
gathered together under the title *The Will to Power*.

I shall quote in finishing the second part of aphorism 289 from
Beyond Good and Evil, which summarizes what I call here the second
Nietzschean function of the mask:

> The hermit does not believe that any philosopher—assuming that
> every philosopher was first of all a hermit—ever expressed his real
> and ultimate opinions in books: does one not write books precisely to
> conceal what one harbors? Indeed, he will doubt whether a philoso-
> pher could *possibly* have "ultimate and real" opinions, whether be-
> hind every one of his caves there is not, must not be, another deeper
> cave—a more comprehensive, stranger, richer world beyond the sur-
> face, an abysmally deep ground behind every ground, under every
> attempt to furnish "grounds." Every philosophy is a foreground
> philosophy—that is a hermit's judgment: "There is something arbi-
> trary in his stopping *here* to look back and look around, in his not

digging deeper *here* but laying his spade aside; there is also something suspicious about it." Every philosophy also *conceals* a philosophy; every opinion is also a hideout, every word also a mask. (229)

5. The Gay Science

The notion of the "gay science," which summarizes and defines the status of philosophy according to Nietzsche, literally associates joy and science. It is naturally not a question here of joy in the strictly psychological sense nor of the science of scientists, but of a gaiety more profound than any mere psychologically motivated joyfulness and a knowledge crueler than any science. Nietzsche's gay science thus evokes a gaiety that has nothing to do with any possible reason to be gay and a knowledge that has nothing to do with any personal interest or benefit that one could expect of science. It constitutes very precisely a philosophical beatitude in which the most lucid and thus the least reassuring knowledge is accompanied by the most euphoric mood—a state of beatitude one can qualify as absolute, since by definition it escapes every eventual counterargument. How, in fact, could one reason against such a gaiety? Nothing worrisome or sad could ever trouble the mood of a philosopher whose knowledge of the worst is invariably caught up in his sentiment of the best. In addition, it would be vain to bring arguments against that which needs no argument to exist: the case of Nietzsche's gay science.

Before we look in detail at what kind of knowledge Nietzschean gay science actually is, it would not be without usefulness to point out immediately that it is a *knowledge*. Elementary remark, but necessary if one really wants to remember that Nietzschean gaiety is not a simple psychological affair but implies knowledge in the most intellectual and theoretical sense of the term—and in an accessory manner that Nietzsche is not only a psychologist but also and principally a great philosopher. Doubtless Nietzsche always placed himself under the sign of Dionysos, the god of wine and drunkenness. Nietzsche's Dionysos, however, is also the god of the most profound and lucid knowledge, always associating the heat of drunkenness with the cold sobriety of knowledge. This sobriety, as much physiological as it is mental, was recognized by Nietzsche at the end of his lucid life, in

Ecce Homo, as one of his most precious and eminent qualities. Nietzschean beatitude is indeed a drunkenness, but not a drunkenness
which would permit one to be delivered from knowledge, to ignore
what is regrettable and deleterious in knowledge, in the manner of
Pascalian *divertissement.* Quite the contrary, it is what gives access to
knowledge, what authorizes the fullness of knowledge (and alone can
authorize it). There is no serious knowledge which can be received in
conscience without the authorization of an absolute beatitude, which,
setting forth no condition for the exercise of bliss, alone imposes no
limitation on the exercise of knowledge. In this, Nietzschean gaiety is
necessarily theoretical—or theorizing—in order to measure itself
against the ample domain of what it is permitted to know without
suffering injury. Reciprocally, Nietzschean knowledge is necessarily
gay; it exists only in proportion to the gaiety which makes it possible.

Rationalism of the Socratic or Platonic type, which Nietzsche criticizes as early as *The Birth of Tragedy,* constitutes the exact reverse of
the gay science. It would be totally vain, as has often been done, to
attribute this criticism to a supposed Nietzschean irrationalism. What
Nietzsche reproaches fundamentally and will always reproach in Platonic rationalism—as in all philosophical forms of the "sad science"—
is not so much that it is removed from art as that it is not gay enough,
and especially not *knowledgeable enough.* It implies a secret prejudice
in favor of ignorance resulting from distress, a "repression" in the
Freudian sense of what one must not know if one is to maintain the
courage to live (knowledge of death and insignificance, principally).
The search for the truth becomes confused here with an escape from
the truth, and that is Nietzsche's only and permanent complaint with
respect to the majority of searches for the truth: they stop paradoxically short of the mark.

To turn now to the content of the Nietzschean gay science, one can
summarily define it by saying that it is the knowledge of the nonsense, of
the insignificance, of the nonsignificant character of all that exists. One
may comment obviously that such a knowledge implies a paradox—
that of being rather a nonknowledge than a knowledge—since Nietzsche's science can be summarized by the totality of the false knowledge
that he rejects (that is, the innumerable versions or variations of the
notion of an inherent meaning to reality). I shall return in a moment to

this apparent paradox and shall point out here only that if Nietzschean knowledge ultimately becomes confused with ignorance, that makes it no less a knowledge—a knowledge of the disillusion of which philosophical knowledge classically consists from Socrates and Plato on: "I know that I know nothing." Nevertheless, the affirmation of the non- sensical character of all reality is the central and invariable point of Nietzschean knowledge. Even though he is worried by this and marks his distance from it, Karl Schlecta was quite right to find here a brutal summary of Nietzsche's philosophy (if indeed one reduces it to what Nietzsche knows and tends to reveal): "Point 1: The world—human beings included—such as it really is 'in truth.' 'In truth' it *has no meaning; it is* nonsense. Nietzsche never tires of presenting this view ceaselessly in ever newer formulas. One could fill a volume with quotations on this subject."[23] Perhaps one must attribute this elementary lucidity, which is largely missing on the part of all the interpreters of Nietzsche, to the simple fact that Schlecta, a philologist first and then a philosopher (just like Nietzsche, one might add), is at least able to read what is written. In any case, the diagnosis proposed here is correct. Nietzsche ceaselessly repeats that any interpretation of the real in terms of signification is an illusion and an aggression against it, that there is nothing "meaningful" or honorable to say on the subject of the world, and that precisely in his refusal to detect in it any meaning resides all the meaning and honor of his own philosophy. Need one invoke here the innumerable pages where Nietzsche develops this same theme in one form or another. This would necessitate, in fact, a large volume, as Schlecta indicates, nearly all Nietzsche's work could conceivably be placed in it. I shall simply recall, for memory's purposes, aphorism 109 of *The Gay Science,* "Let us beware," in which the essential Nietzschean argument on this point is found in condensed form. There is no order which cannot and should not be interpreted as a particular case of general disorder, no regularity which is not an expression among others and with the same validity as others of the absolute fortuitousness to which, in the final analysis, all the law of the world is reduced, that is, its chance, its absence of law.

One cannot fail to ask how this knowledge of the senseless can coexist with the constant Nietzschean affirmation of the *necessity* of the real, a necessity which Nietzsche, following apparently in the foot-

steps of Stoic philosophy, makes into both an intellectual and a moral
dictum as early as *Human, All Too Human:* "You must believe in the
Fatum—knowledge can force you to do so." And in the program for
thought which Nietzsche set out for himself at the beginning of book
four of *The Gay Science* (aphorism 276), one finds that the recognition
and the love of necessity figure prominently: "*Amor fati,* let that be my
love henceforth!" (223). How could that which is absolutely fortuitous be at the same time that which is absolutely necessary? Nietzsche's detractors will not miss the chance to speak here, as well as in
other circumstances, of a major contradiction capable of invalidating
Nietzschean thought. And yet at stake here, as is the case everywhere
else in Nietzsche's thought, is only an apparent contradiction, one that
a distinction in levels of analysis or in the meaning of words will soon
remove. As far as necessity and its problematic relation with fortuitousness is concerned, it suffices to distinguish—as Nietzsche himself invites us to do—between the necessity of the *fact* and the necessity of
the *law*. The necessity of that fact poses no problem and signifies only
the irrefutable character of that which comes into existence, that is, of
the real in general. Only the necessity of the law would be in contradiction with the idea of the fortuitousness of the world. But all of Nietzsche's work tends precisely to criticize the idea of a necessary law, to
show the fragile and anthropomorphic character of the concept of law,
whether it be judicial laws or laws of physics. It would obviously be
necessary to distinguish between the necessity of judicial laws and that
of the laws of physics, but only to recognize ultimately that they are
alike and can both be attributed to a comparable anthropological
phenomenon. The concept of law in the sense of a law of physics
inherits the anthropomorphism of the concept of law in the judicial
sense, from which, moreover, it follows historically. Not that the regularity expressed by a law of physics is in itself an illusion. It is the
interpretation of this regularity in terms of a law of nature which is an
illusion, adding to the fact of regularity, which can be taken as nothing
more than an aleatory result of disorder, a notion of order, I would
almost say of obligation, which is borrowed from the judicial idea of
law. In short, every necessity in the form of a law is rejected by Nietzsche as an anthropomorphic projection; only the necessity of the fact is
"necessary." Nietzsche summarizes his thought on this point very well

when he declares in aphorism 109 of *The Gay Science,* cited earlier, that "the total character of the world, however, is in all eternity chaos—in the sense not of a lack of necessity but of a lack of order . . ." (168). The necessity of which Nietzsche speaks does not mean that the real presents a meaning or an order, but that its chaotic and fortuitous character is nonetheless marked by the seal of the ineluctable, the ineluctable presence of the real, which *suffices* to make of it a necessity understood in terms of order or law. This is almost what Nietzsche expresses at the end of the ninth aphorism of *The Birth of Tragedy:* "That is your world! What a world indeed!" (72 [translation slightly modified]). It is well known that this is a quotation taken from Goethe in the first scene of *Faust.* What Nietzsche does with it, however, is exactly the contrary of the meaning it has in Goethe. In Goethe, Faust, aging and confronted with his books and laboratory retorts, complains of the silence and unintelligibility of the world: "Such is my world: and what a world!"[24] In other words, that *does not suffice,* in Faust's mind, to make a world; there is not enough meaning. For Nietzsche it is the inverse: "That is your world! What a world indeed!" That is enough to make a world; we shall do without meaning.

It remains to clarify how the idea of nonsense constitutes a gay science which is in harmony with Nietzschean beatitude. There is only an apparent difficulty in this, or rather no difficulty at all, to the extent that the idea of nonsense is in Nietzsche completely foreign to a sentiment of disillusion or disabuse. When Nietzsche declares that there is no meaning to be sought in existence, he does not in the least mean that existence is vain and without interest, that there is no "reason to live." The Nietzschean theme of the insignificance of the world designates only the impossibility—in the absence of illusion or betrayal—of recognizing in the world a meaning on the scale of human language or intelligence. Schlecta again puts it quite correctly: "Nietzsche tries in his work to clarify the fact that (a) the world in truth is *without any meaning* and (b) any attribution of meaning up to now has been only a too human intermediary act" (*Le Cas Nietzsche,* p. 113). According to Nietzsche, every meaning is false because it is anthropomorphic, but that does not imply that one is in a position to declare a general absence of meaning in things. Such an affirmation would be vain and contradictory concerning a domain about which one recognizes precisely that one understands nothing. In a like manner, Hume criticizes the idea that people have of causality, of their own subjectivity, of God, but he nonetheless does not deduce from this that "there is no" causality, subjectivity, or God. Such denials would be exactly as absurd as the theses to which they are opposed. Simply, there is *nothing to think*, nothing, that is, nothing which affirms but also necessarily nothing which denies. This is something like what Lacan expressed in his own manner while answering the indiscreet question of a listener who wanted to know whether or not he believed in God. His answer was neither a yes nor a no but the following: "It's curious, but it's completely indifferent to me." Only a priest, before or after being defrocked, can affirm that God does not exist.

6. Nietzsche and Morality

Especially toward the end of the lucid part of his life, Nietzsche expressly centered his work on a critical objective, inviting relentless combat against the whole group of moral judgments held in honor from Plato up to his time, a combat whose victorious outcome as Nietzsche conceives of it should consist in an "inversion of all values." It would be vain to object at this point that Nietzsche did not himself fulfill his own program, because the destruction of values which he proposed to make the subject of his *Will to Power* is already largely accomplished by writings such as *Beyond Good and Evil, The Genealogy of Morals, Twilight of the Idols,* and even *The Birth of Tragedy* (it is in fact a weakness of the plans Nietzsche feverishly lays out in 1887 and 1888 not to announce anything that is really new, and it is difficult to understand the importance attributed to them by many commentators, Heidegger included, to the detriment of texts that were actually written). The question which comes to mind is rather to know whether or not the critical enterprise is indeed the dominant concern of Nietzsche's philosophy, as has been generally thought by Nietzschean (and anti-Nietzschean) posterity, based, it is true, on certain declarations made by Nietzsche himself. Now, this is evidently not at all the case, because it is immediately manifest that the critical concern could not in any case be the principal one in the work of a philosopher whose principal thought, as is evident elsewhere, consists of jubilatory approbation of existence in all its forms. Whatever may be the importance of the critique carried out by Nietzsche, it will necessarily always be secondary—I mean second with respect to the idea of approbation and, moreover, proceeding from it. To make of Nietzsche a thinker essentially concerned with criticizing Christian, Judaic, or Platonic morals is to miss what is "radical" in him, that is, both what interests him in the first place and, second, what is precisely the root and reason for being of the entire Nietzschean critical effort. This is, for example, in my opinion a debatable point in the interpretation of Nietzsche by Gilles Deleuze, which places the full weight of Nietzschean thought in the domain of critical activity, assimilating approbation to a critique of resentment, to a sort of dialectical negation of the negation: "The Dionysian yes is the one which knows how to say no."[25] This interpretation is linked to a general conception of philosophy which Deleuze summarizes thus: "Philosophy as critique reveals the most positive of itself to us—an enterprise of demystification" (*Nietzsche*, 21). All in all this is a very just and penetrating conception, if one takes it generally, that is, in itself, considering only the truth it enunciates and not the truths it excludes. But it is an incomplete and insufficient conception, because the positivity of philosophy—especially if one takes into account the case of philosophers such as Nietzsche—does not consist solely or principally in its critical power, violent though the latter may be, as is the case in Nietzsche and in other thinkers of pure approbation. Critical violence is here a result of another and primary violence, the violence of approbation. And it is toward that and that alone that one must direct questions if one desires explanation of the critical violence it entails.

It is true that the conjugation of approbation and critique is not without posing a grave problem itself. If one looks closely, it seems even to condemn Nietzschean thought to an insurmountable paradox. It contains perhaps the principal internal difficulty of Nietzsche's philosophy, even though this is curiously rather rarely perceived by most of his modern commentators (perhaps because they are able to see only the critical aim of this philosophy). Doubtless one can easily imagine that the philosophy of approbation entails a critique and a disqualification of philosophies suspected of nonaffirmation, especially when the latter, as is almost always the case, cover themselves with the veil of a pseudo-positivity (claiming to speak in the name of the truth, the good, the just, and so on). One cannot fail, however, to ask oneself: If Nietzsche is principally someone who affirms and secondarily someone who criticizes, how does he bring the secondary into harmony with the primary? In what measure is the critical enterprise undertaken by Nietzsche compatible with the Nietzschean principle of unconditional approbation of the real, with the desire, often repeated, never to accuse anything or anyone, not even the accusers, as aphorism 276 of *The Gay Science* states? The solution to the apparent paradox resides in a distinction between two related but different meanings of the notion of *critique.* Today to critique means principally to put into doubt, to contest, to attack, to accuse. This is not at all the meaning of the Nietzschean critical act. To critique also signifies in the first place, according to the Greek and Latin etymology of the term (*Krinô, kriticos, cernere*), to observe, to discern, to distinguish. It is in this primary meaning, which excludes any idea of struggle or combat ("much too polite to argue," Nietzsche said of himself), that Nietzsche is critical—a pitiless observer but with no bad intentions, or without any intention other than that which consists in seeing and understanding and, in an accessory manner, in showing and explaining. Not in order to propose a remedy, to offer a solution for change, nor to step even the slightest bit into the space of "baseness" and of "stupidity" of which Deleuze speaks in his book on Nietzsche. Here one can apply to Nietzsche the letter (although the spirit of the context is different in every respect) of what Descartes declares to be his own philosophical intentions in the second part of the *Discours de la méthode:* "That is why I could in no way approve of those turbulent and restless characters who, although not summoned by birth or fortune to the control of public affairs, are yet constantly effecting some new reform—in their own heads. And if I thought there was the least ground in this work for my being suspected of this madness, I should be very loath to let it be published. My plan has never gone further than an attempt to reform my own thoughts and rebuild them on ground that is altogether my own."[26] This is why recent commentators who attribute to Nietzsche some concern for the struggle against established values, or against whatever it might be, seem to me to have taken a wrong turn. This is notably true of Klossowski, who, as is well known, uncovers in the work of Nietzsche the obsessive project of a plot devised by a very small group of avant-garde intellectuals against the weight of public order and accepted values—without, of course, worrying particularly about the very ideological weight inherent in any small group of intellectuals, as advanced as they might be: "Nietzsche's plot is inconceivable except inasmuch as it would be perpetrated by some small, secret community, imperceptible, which can enter into action under any regime. Only such a community would have the aptitude to disintegrate at the very moment when it projects its action, while it would ineluctably disintegrate in turn as soon as gregarious reality got hold of its secret in an institutional way."[27] In any case, it suffices to reread some of the lines in *Ecce Homo* devoted to the retrospective examination of *Daybreak* to be convinced that Nietzsche had remained for his part, at least for as long as his lucidity was intact, removed from such madness: "With this book my campaign against morality begins. Not that it smells in the least of powder: you will smell far different and much lovelier scents in it, assuming your nostrils have some sensitivity. . . . If one takes leave of the book with a cautious reserve about everything that has so far attained honor and even worship under the name of morality, this in no way contradicts the fact that the whole book contains no negative word, no attack, no spite" (290).

It remains to be seen exactly what the overturning of values toward which Nietzsche was working consists of, what Nietzsche's own morality, or "immorality," consists of in opposition to "traditional" morality. But this is a question already so analyzed and debated that I imagine the reader will appreciate it if I limit myself to a few brief indications.

There is indeed, if one wishes, a "morality" in Nietzsche (with the understanding that it constitutes only a secondary aspect of Nietzschean thought). This morality consists indeed of a sort of overturning of traditional morality—an overturning in the sense that Nietzsche makes sin of virtue and virtue of sin, if I may put it that way, as he says in the following portion of a passage from *Ecce Homo*, quoted earlier, still dealing with *Daybreak*: "This Yes-saying book pours out its light, its love, its tenderness upon ever so many wicked things; it gives back to them their 'soul,' a good conscience, the lofty right and privilege of existence" (290–91). The "virtuous" man according to Nietzsche is the man of beatitude and joyfulness. This is contrary to the ancestral link between joyfulness and delight in sin, as is exemplified, for instance, to cite an illusion taken from modern triviality, by an advertisement once devised for Winston cigarettes: "It's so good it's almost a sin." Joyfulness in all things, but also and primarily joyfulness in oneself, a love of self which revels in all things and would be unable to so revel in the absence of the love which announces a preestablished harmony with the world. Reciprocally, the immoral man in Nietzsche's mind is not only an enemy, generally disguised, of the real; he is primarily an enemy of himself, a *héautontimorouménos,* to use the title of Terence's comedy, an executioner of himself. There is thus a Nietzschean critique of remorse, that is, of the sentiment which designates in the sharpest manner the disharmony of self with self which itself announces a disharmony with any and every object: "Not to perpetrate cowardice against one's own acts! Not to leave them in the lurch afterward! The bite of conscience is indecent" (*Twilight,* 467). This critique, despite appearances, is quite different from the famous critique of remorse carried out by Schopenhauer in *The World as Will and Idea.* Schopenhauer saw in remorse a mistake of conscience which thus believes itself authorized to dissociate itself from its intimate being, that is, its own will. It decides that it should have acted otherwise, but this retroactive wish has no meaning (to act otherwise it would also have been necessary to will otherwise, to dispose of another will, to be another man). For his part, Nietzsche sees in remorse the expression of an indecency, in the sense of Nietzschean morality: loving oneself insufficiently, lacking the indulgence which is one of the absolute rules of love. In Schopenhauer remorse is only an intellectual illusion (even if it has as an effect psychological and moral suffering). In Nietzsche it constitutes a vice.

Just as Nietzschean virtue can be summarized as beatitude and as what one could call a *savoir-jouir,*[28] vice becomes the absence of such a knowledge—and the Latin *vitium,* from which comes the word *vice,* designates precisely a lack, a weakness. The vicious man is the man of nonbeatitude, of nonjoyfulness, of suffering. Suffering is not to be counted in favor of the "vicious" person, according to Nietzsche, since it defines precisely his vice. It is not an attenuating circumstance but rather an aggravating and highly qualifying one, the very circumstance of vice. The suffering of vice is not to be taken in the sense of a simple change in psychological humor, orienting it toward sadness, melancholy, bitterness. It designates more precisely for Nietzsche a passivity, an incapacity to act. The vicious person, according to Nietzsche, is a sufferer to the exact extent that the act he would like to accomplish remains suspended. Thus, it does not suffice to say that he is the man of resentment, the "reactive" man, capable not of action but only of reaction. One must also add that the only reaction of which he is capable is powerless to constitute itself as an act and that in this powerlessness resides his principal motive for suffering and hatred. The analyses of Deleuze on this point are perfectly clear and penetrating, leading to the idea that "resentment is a reaction which ceases to be acted" (*Nietzsche*, 131). The reactive person is indeed and rather paradoxically the one for whom all action, and consequently all true reaction, is lacking; the hateful person is the one who finds himself precisely in a situation where it is impossible to hate (that is, to give to his hatred some expression or form of existence, to make of his hatred an act). In a quite comparable manner, as early as the *Studies on Hysteria,* of 1895, Freud defines repression as the effect not of a bad reaction when faced with a psychologically traumatizing situation but rather of an *absence of reaction* (or of an "abreaction"). It is an effect which adds to the wound the impossibility of being present and responding to it fully, even if only in a pitiful manner. In the same way, Nietzsche defines resentment not as a simple rancor with respect to the real but as an effect combining negativity and passivity. The man of resentment is neither the man of the no nor "the Spirit that denies," as Mephistopheles presents himself in Goethe's *Faust* (46). He is, rather, precisely the spirit who does not succeed in *saying* no and thus who finds himself reduced, in the absence of something better, to mumbling a false yes. This is why the most profound negativity is hunted by Nietzsche not in expressions of the no but in suspicious expressions of the yes—in moral, metaphysical, or ontological discourses, for example, which respectively oppose the concern for good to the joyful partaking of all good things, the concern for a general essence to the joyful partaking of every singular thing, the concern for being to the joyful partaking of every existing thing. In Nietzsche's eyes, these are just so many false yesses which betray the no that they could not or dared not pronounce.

To illustrate in a concrete manner the man of resentment as Nietzsche conceives of him, one can invoke, among thousands of other examples, the case of *Rigoletto,* jester in the court of the Duke of Mantua in the famous opera by Verdi, alias Triboulet in the service of François Ier in *Le Roi s'amuse* by Victor Hugo, the play which inspired Verdi's librettist. Rigoletto is the man promised to resentment simply by his objective situation. He is ugly, deformed, disliked, without power and money among and ordered about by men and women who are beautiful, loved, sought after, powerful, and rich. His resentment, however—and this is why Rigoletto is reactive in the Nietzschean sense—does not consist in a hatred or a negative reaction with respect to life in general and his entourage in particular but rather in the absence of a negative reaction, in his incapacity to express his hatred. One need only scrutinize Verdi's opera to notice the lack of progression and the resulting aggravation of the powerlessness to act of which Rigoletto's resentment precisely consists. Act One: Rigoletto presents himself from the start as one who has renounced the possibility of countering those who counter him and has resigned himself, in the absence of anything better, to courting the courtiers and tacitly approving what they disapprove—in the absence of anything better, because it would have been more effective to attack just a little bit, even if not directly. The solution, which consists in flattering "while waiting"—but waiting for what?—serves as the absolute zero degree of reaction, that is, no reaction. Act two presents a first partial attempt at reaction: Rigoletto suddenly cries out his hatred of the courtiers, whom until then he has ceaselessly flattered. This is an aborted attempt, however, coming at the wrong time (too late) and in the wrong place (Rigoletto accuses the courtiers of having kidnapped his daughter, while they have simply played a joke on him and believe they have kidnapped for a short time his presumed mistress). Better still, Rigoletto comes to regret the imprecation as soon as he utters it and finishes by imploring the pardon and pity of the entourage—in short, by excusing himself for having even seemed to speak when he had no real faculty to do so. The commentary of the entourage is cruel but just, as they remark sotto voce that it is useless to reply to children and to madmen ("fianculli e dementi"), that is, precisely to those who do not yet have or now have lost the faculty of speech. In the third and final act, Rigoletto undertakes a new and ultimate attempt to react, this time in a total and radical manner. He decides to have the Duke of Mantua assassinated, that is, not only the essence of the rich, powerful, and handsome man but also the one for whom his daughter has been kidnapped—double, triple, infinite vengeance after which he will be able to consider himself reimbursed for everything. The event, of course, does not live up to expectations—in spades. Not only will the revenge fail as the duke escapes unharmed but, in addition, Rigoletto's beloved daughter meets her death. The desired event is transformed into an "antievent" which removes all perspective of revenge from the very object which was its principal motivation. Nothing has happened— even something less and something worse than nothing. Therein lies the suffering of Rigoletto, in the fact that this nothing summarizes his entire faculty of reaction. Whatever he says, he will say nothing; whatever he does, he will do nothing. He has a choice only between the same and worse—a worse, moreover, which will soon be confused with the same. What Rigoletto becomes after the murder of his daughter is not revealed by the story, but one could bet heavily that he will take up his service at the court the very next morning—again for lack of something better and probably after offering some new excuses.

I shall point out in closing that the critical enterprise of Nietzsche, which consists essentially in distinguishing the false yesses from the true ones (since no objective criterion allows one to differentiate between them at the level of their manifest expression) presupposes a psychological penetration which is akin to divination, a sort of infallible instinct or flair. Now, Nietzsche flatters himself—rightly or wrongly but in my opinion rightly—in claiming that he possesses such a flair: "My instinct for cleanliness is characterized by a perfectly uncanny sensitivity . . ." (*Ecce Homo*, 233). And he is also right, if indeed Nietzschean critique is to be believable, to identify therein one of his most eminent philosophical virtues: "I was the first to *discover* the truth by being the first to experience lies as lies—smelling them out.—My genius is in my nostrils" (*Ecce Homo*, 326).

7. The Eternal Return

The theme of the eternal return in Nietzsche has given rise to multiple and subtle exegeses on the part of contemporary philosophers, who habitually consider it one of the principal keys to Nietzschean thought, if not its very center. Interpretations of it are varied and often contradictory: return of nothing according to Klossowski,[29] return of the difference inherent in each thing according to Deleuze,[30] return of the Same and as a consequence an attestation of an eternal being transcending every existing thing according to Heidegger.[31] The majority of the interpreters, however, agree at least on the fact that they recognize in the idea of the eternal return one of Nietzsche's master ideas. This unanimity does not suffice, nonetheless, to persuade without hesitation the reader of Nietzsche, who is inevitably led to ask why such a theme, if it is so important, occupies such a materially small part of Nietzsche's work. Heidegger, who founds the essentials of his interpretation of Nietzschean thought on this theme, is himself forced to admit that Nietzsche himself "speaks of it *with parsimony*" (*Nietzsche*, 1.211; Heidegger's emphasis). To my knowledge, only two rather short pages expressly devoted to the question of the eternal return exist in all the books Nietzsche published or whose publication he authorized: aphorism 341 of *The Gay Science* and aphorism 56 of *Beyond Good and Evil*. True, we could not assign a secondary or negligible place to the idea of the eternal return in the work of Nietzsche based solely on the effective rarity of the texts devoted to it, for Nietzsche speaks elsewhere and rather frequently of the great importance that he attributes to this idea, although he does not give a precise description of its nature. It would be vain, I believe, however, to look for the content of this idea in what Nietzsche might have felt about it, in the evening of his lucid life, without ever succeeding in writing anything about it—in what Nietzsche found himself prevented from or "held back" from expressing, as Heidegger invites us to do when he interprets Nietzsche principally from the perspective of all that Nietzsche *did not say* with respect to the eternal return (an empty space which, as we know, Heidegger amply filled with his own concerns and in his own way): "*If our knowledge were limited to what was published by Nietzsche himself, we could never learn what Nietzsche knew already, what he was preparing and nurturing ceaselessly, but what he held back*" (*Nietzsche*, 1.211; Heidegger's emphasis). Research like this gives rise to interpretations all the more suspicious in that they dispense with any text upon which they might be based. And in any case it seems terribly vain to study a thought which was not expressed. A thought is understood by what is written or expressed in some manner or another. Naturally, this does not mean that the opposite is true: what is written is not necessarily thought—far from it. The fact remains, however, that for there to be a thought, its expression is at least a necessary condition if not a sufficient one. The best we can do, then, is to limit ourselves to what Nietzsche wrote and published on the subject of the eternal return, that is, aphorism 56 of *Beyond Good and Evil,* and especially aphorism 341 of *The Gay Science,* which remains both the most developed and the most illuminating text on the question.

Here is the beginning of the aphorism from *The Gay Science:*

> What if some day or night a demon were to steal after you into your loneliness and say to you: "This life as you now live it and have lived it, you will have to live once more and innumerable times more; and there will be nothing new in it, but every pain and every joy and every thought and sigh and everything unutterably small or great in your life will have to return to you, all in the same succession and sequence—even this spider and this moonlight between the trees, and even this moment and I myself. The eternal hourglass of existence is turned upside down again and again, and you with it, speck of dust!" (273)

This beginning is doubly informative. It indicates first and in the clearest manner that the concept of the eternal return corresponds in Nietzsche to a simple *idea,* that is, a supposition, or better yet a fiction ("if a demon were to say to you"). The eternal return is presented from the start (because this is the first text published by Nietzsche on the question) not as a thesis having a bearing on the truth of things but as a hypothesis inviting an affective reaction. In constitutes a *question,* a test, a sort of invitation comparable to but the opposite of the devil's temptation when he dangles before the eyes of the potential sinner a miraculous world, a place of pleasure that is as absolute as it is illusory (while the Nietzschean demon whispers in your ear: What would you say about this world that is yours already, made of pain and tears?). In the second place, the interest of this text is to present—and it is the only one to do so in such a clear manner—a succinct *description* of the eternal return, of its content, to be precise about what exactly returns

according to the Nietzschean idea of the return. What returns—or
rather, would return, because once again it is a question of a fiction, as
it was always a question of a fiction in Nietzsche—is precisely this
world which is already here: "There will be nothing new in it." At
stake is a strict repetition, which nevertheless does not exclude the
return of difference such as Deleuze suggests, if it is the case that life
itself is constituted by differences, but does exclude a return of the
same as it is imagined by Heidegger, since the latter implies a permanence of being transcending all existence in time. It is in this sense, and
not in the one of the vicious circle that Klossowski develops, that the
idea of the eternal return constitutes, as Nietzsche writes at the end of
aphorism 56 of *Beyond Good and Evil,* a *"circulus vitiosus deus"*—to
bring back what has never ceased to be present (68). [Gérard de]
Nerval admirably expresses this coincidence of the elsewhere and the
here in which the secret of the Nietzschean eternal return ultimately
resides in his poem "Delfica":

> Ils reviendront, ces dieux que tu pleures toujours!
> Le temps va ramener l'ordre des anciens jours;
> La terre a tressailli d'un souffle prophétique . . .
>
> Cependant la sibylle au visage latin
> Est endormie encor sous l'arc de Constantin
> —Et rien n'a dérangé le sévère portique.[33]

Here now is the end of aphorism 341 of *The Gay Science:*

> Would you throw yourself down and gnash your teeth and curse the
> demon who spoke thus? Or have you once experienced a tremen-
> dous moment when you would have answered him: "You are a god
> and never have I heard anything more divine." If this thought
> gained possession of you, it would change you as you are or perhaps
> crush you. The question in each and every thing, "Do you desire this
> once more and innumerable times more?" would lie upon your
> actions as the greatest weight. Or how well disposed would you
> have to become to yourself and to life *to crave nothing more fer-
> vently* than this ultimate eternal confirmation and seal? (273–74)

Here the concept of the eternal return fully unveils what remains of its
nature and function—and without ambiguity. The eternal return in
Nietzsche plays the role of a revelation first and foremost. Not a strictly

philosophical revelation about a truth concerning things but rather a psychological one, concerning the truth of human desire. It signals both the optimal desire in those who take the idea of the return lightly—that is, favorably and lovingly—and the weakness of desire in those who feel that such an idea is eminently heavy and weighty. That is, in fact, the title of the aphorism: "The greatest weight." What the eternal return evaluates is the intensity of joy and sadness, respectively, of which it authorizes the "ultimate eternal confirmation," the "ultimate eternal seal." And it is in this sense and in this sense alone, I believe, that the idea of the eternal return effectively constitutes a decisive idea in Nietzsche. The correct reception of the idea of the eternal return is the most indisputable mark of joy in Nietzsche's eyes. He himself defines this idea, in a passage from *Ecce Homo,* as "this highest formula of affirmation that is at all attainable" (295) and the expression of "the Yes-saying pathos *par excellence*" (296). In the same manner, aphorism 56 of *Beyond Good and Evil* describes the man of beatitude as the man of *encore* and of *da capo,* an adept of the eternal return because he wants and would want again without respite what he has and feels. It is also, moreover, the mark of love to be ever more sensitive to the charm of what one loves than to the torment that one happens to suffer from it—always wanting anew one's suffering provided the charm remains, like Masetto in act one of Mozart's *Don Giovanni* when he succumbs for better or worse to the very bad arguments which Zerlina presents to him ("Batti, batti, o bel Masetto"). Thus is defined according to Nietzsche the absolute integrity of joy and of love, always to want anew and always more of the same. And Deleuze is quite right to attribute to the Nietzschean thought concerning the eternal return a fundamentally selective character, apt at recognizing the perfection of desire and the "absolutely good will" (not in the Kantian sense but in the Nietzschean sense): "The eternal return gives to the will a rule as rigorous as the Kantian rule. . . . As an ethical thought, the eternal return is the new formulation of the practical synthesis: *Want what you want in such a way that you would also want its eternal return*" (*Nietzsche,* 77).

The yes which is tested in the idea of the eternal return has a value in that it accepts, or rather would be disposed to accept, the pure and simple return of every existing thing. It is thus characterized by the fact that no complaint, no request for revision, is lodged against the real. It

means adherence to what is, with no reserve in the form of possible or
desirable amendment. Here again the joyful lightness of Nietzsche is
opposed to—and surpasses—the optimism of Leibniz, who nonetheless is rather close to him in many respects. Before Nietzsche, Leibniz's
joy goes all the way to the point of affirming the thought of the eternal
return: "But it will be said that evils are great and many in number in
comparison with the good: that is erroneous. . . . I believe there would
be few persons who, being at the point of death, were not content to
take up life again, on condition of passing through the same amount of
good and evil, provided always that it were not the same kind: one
would be content with variety, without requiring a better condition
than that wherein one had been."[33] This Leibnizian version of the
eternal return is manifestly close to the Nietzschean one. One can
grasp, however, how the eternal according to Leibniz differs from the
eternal return according to Nietzsche and is thus the indication of a
lesser beatitude, if we are to judge in terms of Nietzschean values. If it
is in profound harmony with Nietzsche in demanding nothing better, it
demands nonetheless a slight variation of the same. Now, as we saw
earlier, such a demand does not in the least figure into the Nietzschean
idea of the eternal return: "Everything unutterably small or great in
your life will have to return to you, all in the same succession and
sequence." This is why it is difficult to agree with Deleuze when he
declares that the eternal return in Nietzsche carries out a "second
selection" privileging the return of active forces and eliminating that of
reactive forces: "It suffices to relate the will toward nothing with the
eternal return to understand that reactive forces do not return. As far
as they go and as deep as the becoming-reactive of forces may be,
reactive forces will not return. The small, petty, reactive man will not
return" (*Nietzsche*, 80). The idea of a possible progression of the
good, of a better ready to burst forth within the better itself, would
doubtless win the approval of Leibniz, but certainly not that of Nietzsche. One could hardly see, moreover, upon which Nietzsche texts
such an interpretation could be built, if not on the texts concerning
nihilistic will, which there is no reason to link to the theme of the
eternal return. A passage which is both exhilarating and saddening in
Ecce Homo would sufficiently confirm, if that were still needed, Nietzsche's veiws on this point:

When I look for my most exact opposite, the immeasurable baseness of instincts, I always find my mother and my sister—to believe I am related to such *rabble* would be to blaspheme my divine nature. The manner in which my mother and sister have treated me, even up to this very moment, inspires in me an unspeakable horror. It is a veritable diabolical machine at work and which watches with an infallible sureness for the moment when it can wound me the most cruelly, in my highest moments. . . . For, no force allows me to defend against his venomous vermin. . . . I admit that my most profound objection against the "eternal return," my truly "*abysmal*" thought, is always my mother and my sister.[34]

At stake here is one of the last pages written by Nietzsche several days before his madness declared itself in January 1889 and sent to his printer to be incorporated into the text of the work in extremis, a page that was naturally put aside by Peter Gast, who detected in it, justifiably so, traces of mental illness, and then by Nietzsche's sister, who, in addition, was rather badly treated in it. This page, however, remains quite revealing nonetheless, not only of what Nietzsche thought and had probably always more or less thought of his mother and sister, but especially of what Nietzsche thought and had always thought about the eternal return: that it made (or would make) all things return without distinction, the worst as well as the best.

In the yes tested by the eternal return is tested also the idea of an eternity affecting the whole of what is approved by this yes: the world, life, the self, existence in general. Thus a passage from *Twilight of the Idols* defines "the most profound instinct of life" as "the future of life, the eternity of life" (562). Just as Nietzsche opposes the god of an "eternal yes" toward life to the Christian God in *The Antichrist*.[35] And at the end of one of Nietzsche's poems abundantly analyzed by Heidegger, one finds on this subject an even more general and explicit declaration:

> eternal Yes of being,
> eternally am I thy Yes:
> *for I love thee, O eternity!*[36]

Here there is once again matter for an apparent paradox, since Nietzsche elsewhere unceasingly denounces the will to render things eternal as essentially reactive, as an expression of rancor against life and of a nonsatisfaction with respect to all existence considered as becoming. Thus one has the following passage in *Twilight of the Idols* (but one could invoke on this point numerous other texts): "You ask me which of the philospher's traits are really idiosyncrasies? For example, their lack of historical sense, their hatred of the idea of becoming, their Egypticism. They think that they show their *respect* for a subject when they de-historicize it, *sub specie aeterni*—when they turn it into a mummy" (479). One evidently has the right to be surprised that the desire for eternity, so vigorously criticized by Nietzsche, becomes worthy of praise as soon as beatitude is at stake, or, for that matter, the yes to life as the idea of the eternal return sanctions it. But two different and opposite forms of the desire for eternity must be distinguished here, as a passage from aphorism 370 of *The Gay Science* ("What is romanticism?") makes clear: "The will to *immortalize* . . . requires a dual interpretation. It can be prompted, first, by gratitude and love. . . . But it can also be the tyrannic will of one who suffers deeply, who struggles, is tormented, and would like to turn what is most personal, singular, and narrow, the real idiosyncrasy of his suffering, into a binding law and compulsion" (329–30). Considered from a psychological point of view, the desire for eternity is ambiguous, constituting either a symptom of lack or a sign of plenitude. And, from a philosophical point of view, let us remember that the desire for eternity which Nietzsche recommends affects less the nature of things than the nature of the desire of which he himself, in his own mind, is the most indisputable example. He thus has in mind essentially not a permanence of the world but an insistence of love.

It is well known that the Nietzschean theme of the eternal return constitutes one of the principal arguments of Heidegger, untiringly at work showing that Nietzsche was a thinker concerned above all else with the question of being, who criticized metaphysics of the Platonic type only to better prepare the restoration of a true ontology, who knew how to distinguish between being and the existing thing, that is, who was a proponent of the very philosophy of Heidegger himself: "Nietzsche is among the number of essential thinkers. By 'thinkers' we designate those elected ones among men who have been predestined ever to think only a *single* thought—and that is always 'on the subject of' *the being of the existing thing*" (*Nietzsche*, 1.370). Heidegger thus sees in the idea of the eternal return the obscure intuition of a permanence of being, and invokes in favor of his thesis, for example, a sentence taken from a posthumous fragment collected in *The Will to Power:* "To say that *everything returns,* this is what constitutes *bringing together in the closest proximity the world of becoming and the world of Being: the culmination point of contemplation.*"[37] But he says nothing of the sentence that precedes, describing the production of the world of being as a falsification, and, additionally, he does not find any matter for commentary in the sentence that follows: "The condemnation of becoming, the discontent with regard to it, comes from values attributed to being, once one has begun to invent the world of being" (1.251). Need we say that Heidegger's thesis has a perfect internal coherence and that it finds multiple quotations from Nietzsche upon which it may be based as soon as those quotations are taken from their original context to be integrated into a Heideggerian one. The sole weakness of this interpretation (but it is substantial) is that nothing is more foreign to Nietzsche than the notion of being as Heidegger conceives of it, as everything Nietzsche wrote attests in a vigorous and immediately manifest way. And to ignore the evidence a truly intrepid obstinacy is required, perhaps attributable to what Nietzsche, and before him Schopenhauer, both admired and deplored in the spiritual disposition they themselves qualified as Germanic.

= 3 =

The Cruelty Principle

Introduction

There is probably no well-founded thought possible—and likewise no well-founded work whatever its genre may be, even comedy or *opéra bouffe*—outside the register of the pitiless or of despair (I do not mean by despair a spiritual disposition tending toward melancholy; far from it, rather, a disposition absolutely refractory to anything which resembles hope or expectation). Everything which aims at attenuating the cruelty of the truth, at attenuating the harshness of the real, has the unavoidable consequence of discrediting the most brilliant of endeavors or the worthiest of causes—proof of which can be found, for example, in the cinema of Charlie Chaplin. Concerning this point, I find much perspicacity in a remark by Ernesto Sabato in his novel *Abaddón, el exterminador:* "I want to be cut and dried and to beautify nothing. A theory must be pitiless and turn against its creator if the latter does not treat himself cruelly."

Thinking about this question, I asked myself if one might be able to reveal a certain number of principles governing this "ethic of cruelty," an ethic which, depending on whether it is respected or not, qualifies or disqualifies for me every philosophical work. It seemed to me that this ethic could be summarized in two simple principles, which I call the *principle of sufficient reality* and the *principle of uncertainty,* the exposition of which constitutes the subject of this essay.

1. The Principle of Sufficient Reality

Every philosophy is a *theory of the real,* that is, in accordance with the Greek etymology of the word *theory,* the result of looking at things. This gaze is both creative and interpretive and attempts, in its own manner and according to its own means, to render an account of an object or of a set of given objects. This account can be understood in all senses of the term: an echo or eyewitness report on the one hand (meaning that one draws up a report ȯn such-and-such a subject), a balance sheet on the other hand (meaning that one establishes the sum of the portion one has received in order to be in a position, should the case arise, to render to each person and to each thing the correct change). A philosophical gaze is thus necessarily interpretive by virtue of the simple fact that it "measures," as Nicholas of Cusa suggests so elegantly in *The Layman,* where he relates the mental to the measurable, the act of thinking to the act of measuring. And it is always creative also, since the images of reality that it proposes are not photographs of it but recompositions which differ from the original as much as a novel or a painting might. True, the speculative and intellectual character of philosophy sometimes makes one forget the fabricated, workmanlike aspect of it, which is nevertheless primordial. A philosophy consists first and foremost of a *work,* a creation—a creation whose characteristics do not differ fundamentally from those of any other type of work. Originality, invention, imagination, the art of composition, expressive power are part and parcel of any great philosophical text just as they are of any successful work.

What makes up the specificity of philosophy and distinguishes it from parallel enterprises (art, science, literature) is less the type of technique it mobilizes than the nature of the object it sets out to suggest. That object is not a particular one nor the whole set of particular objects but the whole set of all existing objects, whether or not they are actually present, in short, reality in general conceived in the totality of its spatiotemporal dimensions. The philosopher must give an account not of an act of looking at this or that thing but of looking at every type of thing, including those which are outside his or her field or perception (and these are naturally the most numerous, beginning with the ones which belong to the immediate world but which, because they are already infinitely too numerous, already infinitely exceed the attentive capacities given to human beings and necessarily escape observation). To repeat what Lucretius said: reality is composed on the one hand of this world of which we can on occasion have a partial perception (*haec summa*), and on the other hand of the set of worlds of which we can almost never have any perception (*summa rerum*). The ambition to render an account of the set of known and unknown objects defines both the arrogance and the specificity of philosophical activity. Let me insist: philosophy consists essentially not in being more "theoretical" or "abstract" than any other activity but in being more *general*. Its aim is to be a theory of reality in general and not a theory of this or that particular reality (or set of particular facts), unlike, for example, a painting, a novel, a mathematical theorem, or a law of physics. The same real is indeed always the goal. The only difference is that nonphilosophical "theories" are concerned with its detail, while philosophy—the theory of reality "on the whole"—is principally interested in its entirety.

Now, if one conducts an inquiry into the history of philosophy, one soon perceives that the majority of philosophies have been able to attain their goal—that is, the proposition of a general theory of the real—only on the strange condition of dissolving the very object of their theory, of banishing it to the near nothingness which Plato called the "least being" (*mè on*) suitable for things of the senses, that is, for real things, which supposedly exist only partially and barely. It is as if reality, the detail of which a painter or a novelist can render occasionally and in his or her own way, could by contrast be taken as a whole by philosophy only on the condition that it be contested in its very principle and thus that it find itself relieved of its pretension to be, precisely, reality, nothing but reality, all of reality. This is, moreover, a sentiment shared both by philosophy and by the most ordinary common sense—to believe in a confused way that things are true in their detail, when considered one by one, but doubtful in their entirety, when considered in general. A particular fact must be held to be real, but the whole set of particular facts of which reality is composed can be held to be uncertain; in other words, if it is impossible to doubt anything in its particularity, it is nonetheless possible to doubt everything in general (and philosophy is most often the defender of this position). The real event is recognized as real, but not the sum of events of which it is a part, or rather, is not really a part, since there is a precise perception of the first and only a vague sentiment of the second. This paradox of the certainty of the detail combined with the uncertainty of the whole can be enunciated in mathematical form (paradox of an existing element belonging to a nonexistent set) or arithmetical form (paradox of a unit recognized as equal to one but incapable of producing two if a second unit is added to it). Doubtless it would be admitted without difficulty that there is no reality which is not singular and that there is no generic reality, that only particular dogs exist and no general dog, as nominalist philosophers of the Middle Ages taught. It is, however, more difficult to admit that the sum of singular realities equals a nonexistent or imaginary reality, comparable to the shadows of the cave that Plato suggests in a famous passage of *Republic*.

The most remarkable thing about this ancestral reticence of philosophy to take into consideration the only reality is that, contrary to what one could guess, it results not in the least from a legitimate disarray in the face of the immensity and thus the impossibility of such a task, but rather from an absolutely opposite sentiment. It results from the idea that reality, even if we postulate that it is entirely known and explored, will never deliver up the keys to its own comprehension because it does not itself contain the rules for decoding which would allow us to uncover its nature and meaning. To take only reality into consideration, then, would mean to examine in vain a back whose front will always be unknown, or a double whose original will always remain unknown. Thus philosophy habitually stumbles upon the real not because of its incomparable richness but rather because of its lack of reasons to be, which makes of reality a subject both too ample and too narrow—too ample to be completely embraced, too narrow to be understood. There is in fact nothing in the real, as infinite and unknowable as it might be, which can contribute to its own intelligibility. One is consequently forced to look for its principle elsewhere, to try to find outside the real the secret of the real itself. Thus is born the idea of an intrinsic *insufficiency* of the real, which would be absent, if I may say so and in all the senses of the word, from its own "cause."

The concept of the insufficiency of the real—the idea according to which reality cannot be taken into account philosophically without recourse to a principle external to reality itself (Idea, Spirit, World Soul, and so on) called upon to found and explain it, even to justify it—constitutes a fundamental motif of Western philosophy. And yet the idea of a "sufficiency of the real," what I would call in memory of Leibniz and his principle of sufficient reason the *principle of sufficient reality,* appears to be a major inconvenience in the eyes of all the philosophers. All or almost all: one must naturally make exceptions in the cases of philosophers such as Lucretius, Spinoza, Nietzsche, and even to a certain extent Leibniz himself. The intent to philosophize concerning the real and beginning with it even constitutes for philosophers and for laymen a subject of scorn, a sort of enormous fundamental error reserved for those minds which are perfectly obtuse and incapable of a minimum of reflection. That is the origin of the eternal gibes directed by the majority of philosophers toward those who admit an interest in immediate experience, or admit even that they are satisfied with it. Take Hegel in this remarkable passage from the beginning of *The Phenomenology of the Spirit,* which situates such a mental disposition below even the intelligence level of animals:

> We may answer those who thus insist on the truth and certainty of the reality of objects of sense, by saying that they had better be sent back to the most elementary school of wisdom, the ancient Eleusinian mysteries of Ceres and Bacchus; they have not yet learnt the inner secret of the eating of bread and the drinking of wine. For one who is initiated into these mysteries not only comes to doubt the being of things of sense, but gets into a state of despair about it altogether; and in dealing with them he partly himself brings about the nothingness of those things, partly he sees these bring about their own nothingness. Even animals are not shut off from this wisdom, but show they are deeply initiated into it. For they do not stand stock still before things of sense as if these were things *per se,* with being in themselves: they despair of this reality altogether, and in complete assurance of the nothingness of things they fall-to without more ado and eat them up. And all nature proclaims, as animals do, these open secrets, these mysteries revealed to all, which teach what the truth of things of sense is.[1]

This depreciation of immediate reality is a particularly eloquent expression of the "principle of insufficient reality," which constitutes the *credo* shared in common by every philosophical denegation of the real. This is, in addition, a rather comic expression of it, because Hegel suggests here the assimilation of the appetite of animals to the recognition of the ontological poverty of the food they are about to devour, as if it were necessary to persuade the pig of the thinness of the real in the slop one offers it, of the "complete assurance of the nothingness of things," in order to persuade the pig to eat it.

It is in a similar spirit that a modern Hegelian, Eric Weil, believes he is authorized to declare from the very beginning of an article devoted precisely to reality ("On Reality") that the reality we can experience is bereft of all "real reality": "What is given immediately is not real." One could declare with just as much daring that a drink which presents itself to be consumed it not a real drink, or that a woman who offers herself to one's caresses is not a real woman. Such remarks are naturally insane, but they are also, I would claim, highly "philosophical"—in a rather regrettable sense of the term which, as Laurent-Michel Vacher suggests in a recent essay, would readily incite one to think that the principal function of philosophy is "to accredit stupidity while discrediting evidence."[2] We are in fact forced to admit that philosophy, which proposes as its task to understand and interpret what exists, often has eyes and ears only for what does not exist. Nothing could be more surprising ultimately than this common and obstinate penchant of philosophy always to prefer refuting what is manifestly true, thus depreciating instinctively what is clearly agreeable (the latter being the obligatory result of the former, since the suspicion regarding the real extends necessarily to the pleasant experiences the real offers). Spinoza summarizes very well this habitual propensity of philosophy for the inversion of truths and values: "Superstition . . . seems to affirm that what brings sorrow is good, and, on the contrary, what brings joy is evil" (*Ethics,* 31, 450).

The reasons invoked by most philosophers who contest the real, who cast suspicion on the fact of its simple and total reality, have always seemed to me both unconvincing and very suspicious in themselves. Not that such reasons are impertinent, for it is undeniable that reality, unable to explain itself by itself, is in a certain way and forever unintelligible; but to be unintelligible does not mean to be unreal, in the same way that a lover who behaves incomprehensibly still exists, as the most banal of amorous experiences attests daily. The only but very great weakness of philosophical arguments tending to put the full and entire reality of the real in doubt is that they dissimulate the true difficulty of taking into consideration the real and only the real—a difficulty which, if it resides secondarily in the incomprehensible character of reality, resides primarily and principally in its painful character. In other words, I strongly suspect that the philosophical contention with the real originated not in the fact that reality is inexplicable if one appeals only to it but <u>rather in the fact that it is *cruel*</u>. Consequently the idea of sufficient reality, depriving human beings of all possibility of distance or recourse with respect to the real, constitutes a permanent risk of anguish, and of intolerable anguish—as soon as a contrary circumstance arises, a funeral, for example, which renders reality suddenly unbearable, or even in the absense of any particular circumstance, when one suddenly and lucidly looks at reality in general. "Melancholic hypochondria," remarked Gérard de Nerval in a notebook. "It is a terrible affliction—it makes one see things as they are."

By the <u>"cruelty" of the real I mean</u> first of all, obviously, the intrinsically painful and tragic nature of reality. I shall not expand on this first meaning, more or less known by all, and about which, in addition, I have had other occasions elsewhere to speak more abundantly.[3] Let me just recall here the insignificant and ephemeral character of everything in the world. I also mean by the cruelty of the real, however, the unique and consequently the irredeemable and final character of this reality—a character which forbids one both from holding it at a distance and from attenuating its rigor by taking into consideration some kind of instance which might be exterior to it. *Cruor,* from which *crudelis* (cruel) as well as *crudus* (not digested, indigestible)[4] are derived, designates torn and bloody flesh, that is, the thing itself stripped of all its ornaments and ordinary external accoutrements, in this case skin, and thus reduced to its unique reality, as bloody as it is indigestible. Thus reality is cruel—and indigestible—as soon as one removes from it everything which is not reality in order to consider it in itself. Like a condemnation to death which would coincide with its execution, depriving the condemned of the necessary interval during which to present an appeal for mercy, reality ignores and always cuts short every request for an appeal. In the same way that what is cruel in capital punishment is, on the one hand, to be condemned to death and, on the other hand, to be executed, what is cruel with respect to the real is somehow double: to be cruel on the one hand, to be real on the other. With one notable difference: in the case of the death sentence, the execution does not necessarily immediately follow the condemnation, whereas in the case of reality the execution automatically follows the condemnation in such a way that they are one; reality situates its sentence at the very level of execution from the start. A mental distinction remains possible here, even though it is impossible to make such a distinction at the level of the facts. I mean that one can rather ordinarily, and even to a certain extent rather reasonably, consider that reality is cruel by nature, but also, and in a sort of ultimate refinement of cruelty, truly the real. This is more or less what Proust expresses at the beginning of *Albertine disparue:* it is already very sad that Albertine left me with bags all packed, but the worst is to think that all of this is *true* (Proust comments on this distinction by writing that "suffering knows more about psychology than psychology";[5] to my mind he could have said more exactly that suffering knows more about reality than any representation or anticipation one can have concerning it). One of my acquaintances prone to depression regularly expresses his problems in a comparable and highly significant form, even though this may appear to be an absurd tautology: he complains not only that existence is horrible in his opinion but especially that he is *right* to believe this. Not only is the truth hideous, he declares in substance during his depressive moments, but, in addition, it is true that this is so; reality is *indeed* hideous. He could accept the fact that reality is sad, but what really afflicts him and exceeds all measure is the supplemental torment which comes from the idea that a sad truth is simultaneously, adding insult to injury, a *true truth*. In other words, an unbearable reality is also, in an ultimate refinement of cruelty, a real reality. This is just what I wanted to suggest by evoking the double cruelty of the real: it seems that what is most cruel in reality lies not in its intrinsically cruel character but in its ineluctable character, that is, undeniably real.

Let me add in passing that, as with many tautologies, the distinction between "true" and "true truth" or between "reality" and "real reality" is not barren but very fertile in lessons. It illustrates in a general manner the human faculty to live in illusion which is defined in every case by the fact that it makes two things of one, that it introduces an effect of infinite redundancy into everything which presents itself as simple and unique. Thus my depressive acquaintance, who affirms that he sees everything in black but adds that he is right to see everything in black, should add in addition that he thinks he is right to be right, and then that he is right to think that he is right to be right, and so forth. This is like any person living in illusion, moreover, who will always add to the declaration of a particular truth the declaration of a more general truth, which supposedly comforts him, then a third truth to support the second, then a fourth truth to bolster the third, and so on indefinitely. Thus it goes perhaps with anyone who takes the trouble to render an account to his or her desire or repulsion: this adds a worthless commentary which supposedly explains a fact of which it is only a doubled and tautological expression, commonly accompanying every manifestation of love or aversion. Just as the connoisseur of melons insists upon explaining her taste by appealing to a knowledge of the excellent nature of melons, the person who does not like them explains his aversion by appealing to a knowledge of their execrable nature. I like melons, declares the connoisseur of melons, and that's lucky, because otherwise I wouldn't eat them—what a shame that would be! I do not like melons, declares the other person, and that's lucky, because otherwise I would eat them—how horrible! The illusion common to the two cases, as in all cases of illusion, consists in judging that a reality does not suffice in itself and can impose itself only through the denegation of its opposite, or that a fact exists only by virtue of its being restated (which is most often equivalent to the same type of denegation of its contrary), when in fact the essence of the real is precisely to be removed from all contradiction as well as from all possibility of repetition.

To return to my subject, I shall thus say that reality (and I repeat if one takes reality alone in its sufficiency), which already surpasses the human faculty for understanding, also surpasses—and this is more dangerous than the first point—the human faculty for being affected. It should be noted, indeed, that if the intellectual faculty for understanding and the psychological faculty for accepting are equally limited and ultimately impotent in mankind, the lack of the second is infinitely more weighty than that of the first. Being incomprehensible, reality is only a bothersome thing which occasionally troubles the mind but does not interfere with the ordinary exercise of life. Thus everyone becomes habituated without undue difficulty to time, space, movement, even though these are notions which certainly are intimately connected to the real, but also notions which no one has ever been capable of conceiving or defining. Things are quite different with reality, however, as soon as it is experienced as intensely painful. In that case it is opposed by an *intolerance* on the part of the person it affects, while it provokes only a simple and passing state of perplexity in the person who is powerless to understand it. In other words, and to repeat myself, reality, if it indeed exceeds the human faculty of comprehension, has another and principal quality: it exasperates the human faculty of tolerance. When intelligence finds itself overwhelmed by reality, it is usually satisfied by a vague compromise with the real, by a delay and a request for more ample information, even if these are to be deferred eternally. On the contrary, caught in the same trap of the real, affectivity retreats and declares a forfeit, like a resistor, in the electrical sense of the term, which blows out when too much current passes through it. This is exactly what happens to Swann in *Un amour de Swann* when he reaches the point of envisaging the hypothesis that the woman he loves is a strumpet, a hypothesis which, having the weakness of coinciding precisely with reality, is as a result immediately repressed with the help of what Proust indeed describes as a sudden and providential "interruption in electrical current": "He could not develop this idea because a spiritual laziness which was congenital, intermittent, and providential intervened at that moment to turn out all the lights of his intelligence, as abruptly as would later be the case, after electric lighting had been installed everywhere, when the electricity was cut off in a house" (1, 264). In the case of a grave conflict with the real, the man who feels instinctively that the recognition of this real would exceed his power and put his very existence into danger is forced to decide on the spot either in favor of the real or in favor of himself, because there is not a moment to lose: "It's him or me." Ordinarily he grants preference to himself and thus condemns the real, like Swann in the passage just quoted. True, he can also grant prefer-

ence to the real—the case of suicide, whether psychological suicide or
actual suicide.

The acceptance of the real presupposes, then, either pure unconscious-
ness—like Epicurus' pig, who is the only one at ease on board as the
storm rages and fills the passengers and crew with anguish—or a consciousness which would be capable both of knowing the worst and of
not being mortally affected by this knowledge of the worst. It must be
noted that this last faculty—to know without receiving mortal
damage—is situated absolutely *out of reach* of human faculties, unless
of course some extraordinary assistance appears, what Pascal calls
grace and I call for my part joy. Indeed, knowledge constitutes for
humankind a fatality and a sort of curse already recognized in Genesis
("You shall not eat from the tree of knowledge"). Since it is both inevitable (impossible to ignore completely what one knows) and inadmissible
(equally impossible quite to admit it), it condemns humanity. Man is the
being who has ventured into the recognition of a truth which he is
incapable of facing (like a foolhardy general who throws himself into
the assault without being assured of the state of the forces at play and
the possibilities of retreat) and which is a contradictory and tragic
destiny—tragic in the sense that Vladimir Jankélévitch understands it
("the alliance of the necessary and the impossible"). What is most crucial and most notable in what is called the human condition seems to me
to reside precisely in this: to be equipped with a knowledge—contrary
to what is true of animals and inanimate objects—but simultaneously
to be stripped of sufficient psychological resources to confront one's
own wisdom, to be furnished with a surplus of knowledge or with "one
too many eyes," as André Green would say, which indiscriminately is
our privilege and our ruin, in short, to know but to be completely
incapable. Thus, man is the sole creature known to be conscious of his
own death (and of the death promised for all things), but also the only
one to reject without appeal the idea of death. He knows that he is living
but knows not how he lives; he knows he must die but knows not how
he will die. In other words, man is the being capable of knowing what he
is incapable of knowing, of being able in principle to do what he is
incapable of doing in reality, of finding himself confronted precisely
with that which he is incapable of confronting. Equally incapable of
knowing and of ignoring, he demonstrates contradictory capacities

which prevent the formulation of all plausible definitions of him, as Pascal insists in the *Pensées*. One could say that a divine and universal programmer (unless it is just a chance combination of things, as Epicurus suggests) committed in this instance a basic error, sending confidential information to a terminal which was not in a state to receive it, to master it, and to integrate it into its own program, revealing to humanity a truth that we are incapable of admitting but also, unhappily, very capable of understanding. This is why Lucretius' poem, which sets out to cure human anguish by revealing the truth, can only have as its principal result to increase that very anguish. To administer the truth to one who suffers precisely from the truth is worthless. In the same manner, the forced perception of reality to which Lucretius invites us is without benefit for someone who fears above all reality taken in itself, in its unadorned and cruel state. The cure is worse than the disease here. Exceeding the powers of the afflicted person, it can only treat a cadaver which has already succumbed to the test of a real which was beyond its capacities—or occasionally comfort someone who is well and has no need of comfort. In a passage from his *Zibaldone*, Leopardi perfectly analyzes this inadequacy and necessary contradiction which opposes the exercise of life to the knowledge of life:

> One can hardly better expose the horrible mystery of things and universal existence . . . than by declaring insufficient and even false not only the extension, the influence, and the force, but the fundamental principles of our reason themselves. The principle, for example—without which every proposition, every discourse, every argument, and the capacity to be able to establish and conceive the truth collapses—the principle, as I was saying, according to which *a thing cannot simultaneously both be and not be* seems absolutely false when one considers the palpable contradictions which exist in nature. To exist in fact and to be unable in any way to be happy, by virtue of an innate impotence inseparable from existence, or rather, to be and to be unable not to be unhappy, are two truths as proven and as certain with respect to man and to every living being as any truth can be according to our principles and our experience. Now, a being united with unhappiness, and united with it necessarily and by its essence, is something which is in direct contradiction with itself, with perfection and its very goal which is happiness alone, a thing which ravages itself, which is its own enemy. Thus the being of living beings is in a natural, essential, and necessary contradiction with itself.[6]

Cioran briefly summarizes the same thought in an aphorism from *The Temptation to Exist:* "To exist is to protest against the truth."[7]

Thus normally one can live only on the condition that one keep the truth at bay, or rather, that one continually approach it at cross-purposes—an exhausting task illustrated by the ancient myth of Sisyphus among others. This is also illustrated by the majority of philosophical enterprises whose principal aim is not to reveal the truth but indeed to make us forget it, to disguise its cruelty and make it into a remedy which temporarily eases the pain, to soften the confrontation with reality by an infinite variety of cures, more or less improvised according to whether the philosopher has more or fewer mental resources. Such enterprises are always ultimately a hallucinatory exorcism of the real, similar to the naive declaration by Eric Weil evoked earlier ("What is given immediately is not real"). The philosopher—I repeat, not all philosophers, but a great number of them—is like a doctor at the sickbed of someone with an incurable illness, careful to relieve the suffering at any price (suffering which he or she shares, moreover), but indifferent to the value of the means put to use provided they have a tangible and immediate effect. The philosopher's first concern is thus to try, whatever the cost may be, to establish that the real is not the real, since it is the real from which one suffers and which is ultimately the root of all evil. Likewise, Marcel Proust, upon learning that Albertine has left, finds a remedy as instinctive as it is absurd in the idea that Albertine has not really left:

> These words, "Mademoiselle Albertine has left," had just produced in my heart such suffering that I felt I would not be able to resist it very long; I had to make it stop immediately. Gentle with myself as my mother had been with my dying grandmother, I told myself with the same goodwill that one displays when one does not want the thing one loves to suffer: "Be patient for a moment, a remedy will be found, be calm, we won't let you suffer like that." And confusedly guessing that if indeed a minute ago when I had not yet rung the departure of Albertine had appeared indifferent to me, even desirable, because I believed it to be impossible, that was the kind of idea that my instinct chose to put on my open wound, the first balm: "All of that has no importance, because I am going to make her come back immediately. I am going to examine all the means, but in

any case she will be here this evening. Consequently, it's not worthwhile torturing myself." (4.3).

Clearly one can replace the formula "Mademoiselle Albertine has left"
with the formula "the real is the real" without having to change a
single other word in this passage of *Albertine disparue*. Thus philosophy is generally obstinate in replacing the idea that "this is" by the
idea that it is impossible and inadmissible that "that be," opposing the
fantastic and moral reign of a "must be" to the sovereign and confin-
ing reign of being.

Since I am evoking in incidental fashion the human (and philosophical) propensity for moralism, I shall profit from the moment to
repeat a truth which I have already expressed in a work of my
youth:[8] what morality fights against is not at all the immoral, the
unjust, the scandalous, but indeed the real—the sole and true source
of scandal. The case of Plato and Rousseau, to limit my remarks only
to these two eminent specialists of moral questions, is very enlighten-
ing here. The deviousness of Plato consists in fact in constantly representing as reprehensible and unworthy of human beings what constitutes, on the contrary, our highest and most difficult task, that is, to
accept the real, to find satisfaction in the sensual and perishable
world. Likewise, the madness of Rousseau consists essentially in con-
demning as immoral every reality if it is tragic. Rousseau, who never
claims this absurd idea as his own even though he is constantly
fascinated by it, baldly admits to it, however, owing probably to a
moment of inattention, in a striking passage of his *Letter to M.
d'Alembert*:

> What do we learn from *Phèdre* and Oedipe other than that man is
> not free and that heaven punishes him for the crimes it makes him
> commit? What do we learn in *Médée*, other than how cruel and
> unnatural a mother can be made by the rage of jealousy? Look at
> most of the plays in the French theater; in practically all of them you
> will find abominable monsters and atrocious actions, useful, if you
> please, in making the plays interesting and in giving exercise to the
> virtues; but they are certainly dangerous in that *they accustom the
> eyes of the people to horrors that they ought not even to know and
> to crimes they ought not to suppose possible.* (my emphasis)[9]

In other words, it is immoral and shocking to reveal the truth to whomever, since the truth is unpleasant. Put another way, the truth is admissible accompanied by a certain degree of cruelty, beyond which it is forbidden. The final meaning of Plato's philosophy as well as of Rousseau's thus seems to me to be summarized by this simple and aberrant adage: if the truth is cruel, this is because it is false, and it must consequently be both refuted by learned individuals and hidden from the people. Kant seems to me often to be inspired by the same adage, purposefully basing—or believing that he is basing—the validity of the theses which are important to him (such as the immortality of the soul or the rationality and the finality of nature) on the sole consideration of the disagreeable character of the inverse hypotheses. Thus, one has this strange demonstration of the first proposition from *The Idea of a Universal History on a Cosmo-Political Plan.* Proposition: "All tendencies of any creature, to which it is predisposed by nature are destined in the end to develop themselves perfectly and agreeably to their final purpose."[10] Demonstration: "Once departing from this fundamental proposition, we have a nature no longer tied to laws, but objectless and working at random; and a cheerless reign of chance steps into the place of reason" (4). True ideas are ultimately easily separated from false ideas for Kant: the former are recognizable by their agreeable nature, the latter by their "deplorable" aspect.

One feels like replying that if reality can indeed be cruel, it is no less real all the same. Dura lex sed lex: realitas crudelis sed realitas. The harshness of the thing does not prevent the thing from being, perfectly indifferent to those it tortures and can even destroy on occasion. The experience of reality is thus comparable to the cruelty mixed with gaiety of which Nietzsche speaks in "The Case of Wagner" when he talks about Bizet's *Carmen:* "This music is cheerful, but not in a French or German way. Its cheerfulness is African; fate hangs over it; its happiness is brief, sudden, without pardon" (158). This observation by Nietzsche holds for all reality, whether it be experienced as gay or sad. It is well known, moreover, that the quality of being "without pardon" (*ohne Pardon*), which Nietzsche grants precisely to Bizet's music in *Carmen,* is in everyday language linked to a fatal event or decision. Happiness and sadness share the common destiny of every experience of reality, to be immediate and only immediate. And the fatality which floats above reality, as Nietzsche says, signifies not that it is the result of a destiny inscribed in advance, but only that its immediacy makes it both ineluctable with respect to its presence at the moment and more than uncertain with respect to its chances of duration or survival. Need one recall that the ineluctable designates not what would be necessary for all eternity but what is impossible to avoid at this very moment?

Moral thought and tragic thought are thus rivals in our minds, suggesting to us in turn the most comforting but the most illusory idea (the principle of insufficient reality) and the most cruel but the truest idea (the principle of sufficient reality). There are thus two great categories of philosophies and philosophers according to whether they call for a better or, on the contrary, make do with the worst. This is a little like what Samuel Butler suggests in a passage from *The Way of All Flesh:* "Very few care two straws about truth, or have any confidence that it is righter and better to believe what is true than what is untrue, even though belief in the untruth may seem at first sight most expedient. Yet it is only these few who can be said to believe anything at all; the rest are simply unbelievers in disguise."[11] Personally, I would propose to distinguish between two sorts of philosophers: the species of philosopher-healers and that of philosopher-doctors. The former are sympathetic and ineffective, the latter effective and pitiless. The first have nothing solid to counteract human anguish, but they dispose of a gamut of false remedies which can lull anguish to sleep for more or less time; they are not capable of curing people, but they suffice, I would say, to keep them just barely alive. The second dispose of the true remedy and the only vaccination (I mean the administration of the truth), but it is so strong that if indeed it occasionally comforts healthy natures, its other and principal effect is to make weak natures perish on the spot. This is, moreover, a paradoxical and remarkable fact, although little noted as far as I know (and as true of medicine as of philosophy), namely, that they are effective only for those who are not sick, for those who dispose of a certain minimum degree of health. In the same way that a philosophy is heard and understood only by those who actually almost knew it beforehand and thus do not really need it, medicine can and will ever be able to cure only healthy people.

2. The Principle of Uncertainty

> The craving for a strong faith is no proof of a strong
> faith, but quite the contrary. If one has such a faith,
> then one can afford the beautiful luxury of skepticism.
> —Nietzsche, *Twilight of the Idols*

In a passage from *In Defense of Raymond Sebond,* Montaigne suggests a definition of philosophical truth as unexpected as it is pertinent:

> I can't really convince myself that Epicurus, Plato, and Pythagoras
> have given us as real coin of the realm their atoms, their ideas, their
> numbers. They were too wise to establish their articles of faith on
> something so uncertain and so debatable. But, in this obscurity and
> ignorance of the world, each of these great personages strove to
> bring some suggestion of light, and they directed their intelligence to
> inventions which might have at least a clever and pleasant appear-
> ance, if only, however false, they could be defended against contrary
> presentations.[12]

In other words, the truth set forth by philosophers, their most crucial truth, the one which has served for thousands of years to designate and to characterize their thought, is at the same time a truth of which none of them would be in the least disposed to be the guarantor or "author," in the Latin sense of *auctor*. I would briefly recall here the Latin etymology of the word *author*, the term *auctor* meaning both guarantor and producer. Now, here is a case where the producer in question, namely, the philosopher, demonstrates the greatest circumspection with regard to his own best productions: Pythagoras does not believe in numbers, Plato does not believe in ideas, Epicurus does not believe in atoms. Unlike the fanatic, he possesses sufficient wisdom not to defend to his last breath a truth which he did indeed assert, but which he also knows probably better than anyone else to be largely doubtful—as Montaigne suggests in still another passage of the *Defense:* "Indeed, I do not know whether the ardor which is born of vexation and stubbornness in facing the imposing power and violence of authority and of danger, or the interest of his reputation, has not persuaded many a man to support, even at the risk of his life, an opinion for which among his friends and at liberty, he would not have been willing to lift a finger" (82).

The fact that a philosopher is less persuaded than anyone else of the truth of what he or she claims may seem highly paradoxical. The fact is nonetheless indubitable and is the result of the very nature of philosophical "truth." One can naturally and justifiably observe that it is in the nature of every truth, of whatever type, to be doubtful. Thus every fact, as simple and as evident as it might be at the moment of its occurrence, becomes uncertain and vague as soon as the event, now past, is summoned before the tribunal of justice or collective memory. In the same way, a scientific truth, as certain as it might seem at a given moment, is quickly worn out by contact with later conceptions which interpret it in another fashion, in the context of a new theory which radically modifies its terms. Thus, strictly speaking, there are no "exact sciences" (with the exception of mathematics, which renounces all factual truth and is satisfied with making conclusions agree with premises). Just like a historical truth, a truth of physics is forever subject to suspicion and revision. All the same, the historian and the physicist evoke indubitable facts, even if they are incapable of proposing a sure and definitive version of them. The interpretations of the French Revolution or of the law of gravity are and perhaps will always remain more or less contested, but it is impossible to doubt the fact, to think, for example, that the French Revolution did not take place or that gravity corresponds to nothing that is observable in nature. The one and the other are true: the first when it took place, the second when it was conceived. They are true to the extent that they were true in their time and can thus claim, as Hegel would say, a certain "moment" of truth. Now, the essence of philosophical truths, contrary to other types of truth, is that they are never able to claim a similar "moment of truth." To the extent that philosophy is a science of unsolvable problems, or at least of unresolvable problems, as [Léon] Brunschvicg was fond of saying, the solutions it brings to its own problems are necessarily and by definition doubtful—to such an extent that a truth which would be certain would cease for that very reason to be philosophical truth. And a philosopher who would be persuaded of the truth he or she proposes would cease in that same moment to be a philosopher (while it can happen, by contrast, that the philosopher can be persuaded in a reasonable way of the falsity of the theses he or she is criticizing). This principle of uncertainty, according to whether it is respected or not, can, moreover, serve as a criterion to distinguish true philosophers from false ones. A great thinker is always extremely circumspect with regard to the value of the truths he or she suggests, while a mediocre philosopher can be recognized, among other things, by the fact that he or she remains firmly persuaded of the truth of the inept ideas he or she asserts.

One can naturally ask oneself whether there is any interest in a philosophical truth necessarily destined to be doubted and uncertain and, consequently, lacking all the traditional attributes of the truth. It should be noted here first of all that the interest an idea presents is never to be confused with certain knowledge of its truth, no more than the interest presented by a fact is to be confused with the knowledge of its nature. Thus the fact of sexuality and of universal expression of interest in it has always coexisted easily with its highly obscure and incomprehensible character, which has been admitted in all sincerity by those who have tried the hardest to pierce its mysteries: Freud, Georges Bataille, Lacan, and before them Schopenhauer. From this one can deduce precisely that, like all profound truth, every interesting reality is basically ambiguous, if not frankly paradoxical, being both recognized by everyone and unknown to anyone in particular. The principal interest in a philosophical truth, however, consists of its negative virtue; I mean by that its power to banish ideas which are much more false than the truth it announces *a contrario*. This is the virtue of a critique which, even if it does not in itself elaborate any clear truth, succeeds at least in denouncing a great number of ideas wrongly held to be true and evident. The quality of philosophical truths is a little like that of erasers used for blackboards: all we ask of them is to erase well. In other words, a philosophical truth is essentially of a hygienic order; it procures no certainty, but it protects the mental organism against the whole family of germs which disseminate illusion and madness. And yet this very uncertainty inherent in philosophical truths, which, if you like, defines their weakness, also defines their force. The act of doubting, in fact, is effective only on what is presented as certain and assured; by contrast, it is totally ineffective against what presents itself as uncertain and doubtful. An uncertain truth is also and necessarily an *irrefutable* truth, doubt being powerless against doubt. This is precisely why Montaigne writes, in the passage quoted earlier, that the essence of every great philosophical "invention" is to "be defended against contrary presentations." A well-founded thought is in fact a thought capable of being defended, not only against all "oppositions" that can be devised, but in addition, and I would say especially, against every enterprise of denaturation and erroneous interpretation—as Samuel Butler says excellently in a passage from *Life and Habit:* "Unless a matter be true enough to stand a good deal of misrepresentation, its truth is not of a very robust order. . . ."[13] Likewise, translations, as terrible as they often are, succeed only in lessening the expressive power of the text they translate but not in canceling it completely, provided the original text is one of quality. This is, moreover, the infallible sign of the quality of a text, namely, always to resist, at least partially, the trial of translation/ betrayal.

I would note in passing that the uncertain character of the profoundest philosophical truths allows us to explain the apparently paradoxical and enigmatic fact that formally opposite and even contradictory propositions can be held to be equally pertinent. Nothing could be more correct, respectively, than what Plato says of love in the *Symposium* and Lucretius in *De rerum natura,* but also nothing as diametrically opposite. This peaceful coexistence of opposite truths can be explained not by a Hegelian fanaticism for an absolute knowledge aiming in the end to reconcile all philosophical truths, but by the uncertain character of each of these enunciations. Considered as definitively proven, philosophical truths are necessarily mutually exclusive since they do not say the same thing. Considered, on the contrary, as doubtful approximations, they are reciprocally tolerant. There is in addition no reason to interpret divergences of doctrine in terms of opposition, to consider that one idea is contradictory to another when it is only *different* from it. Nietzsche notes at the beginning of *Beyond Good and Evil* that the obligatory passage from the idea of difference to the idea of contradiction constitutes one of the principal dogmas of illusion:

> The fundamental faith of the metaphysicians is *the faith in opposite values.* It has not even occurred to the most cautious among them that one might have a doubt right here at the threshold where it was surely most necessary—even if they vowed to themselves, *"de omnibus dubitandum. . . ."* It might even be possible

that what constitutes the value of these goods and revered things is
precisely that they are insidiously related, tied to, and involved
with these wicked, seemingly opposite things—maybe even one
with them in essence." (10)

To return to the fact that philosophical truth has a value only inasmuch as it is uncertain and ultimately possesses no indisputable virtue
other than a medicinal one, I shall briefly invoke the case of the materialism of Epicurus and Lucretius. Indeed, it is self-evident—and this is
why Epicurean doctrine is philosophically exemplary—that this materialism is simultaneously untenable and salutary. It is untenable with
respect to its own truth but salutary with regard to the sum of errors
and absurdities it revokes. The two fundamental maxims of Epicure-
anism can rightly appear to be particularly brief and barren thoughts.
To assimilate the truth to material existence, the good to the experience of pleasure, certainly means to preclude any attempt at elucida-
tion in depth and to remain on these two points at the most minimalist
level of discourse. One must observe, however, that the attempt to
assimilate the truth to anything other than matter, the good to anything other than pleasure, generally leads to assertions which are themselves much more suspicious and absurd than the Epicurean formulas.
As critical philosophy, materialism constitutes perhaps the most ele-
vated thought possible; as "true" philosophy it is on the contrary the
most trivial of all thought. As Nietzsche remarks in a passage from the
ninth aphorism of *Beyond Good and Evil,* which directly echoes Montaigne's proposition quoted earlier, a philosophy ceases to be credible
as soon as it begins to believe in itself. The strength of Epicurean
philosophy, as is the case with any great philosophy, is not to arrive at
a profound and certain truth but, if I may put it this way, to succeed in
remaining at the level of *the least error.* For my part, I see no reason
not to subscribe to the declaration of faith announced by one of G. K.
Chesterton's characters (even though the author is careful to keep his
distance from it as soon as he writes it): "If one must be a materialist
or a lunatic, I choose materialism." And I would add that if a doubtful
truth is preferable to an apparently certain truth, this is also because
the latter inclines more than the former toward the madness which
consists in wanting to obtain universal assent, by force if need be. A
doubtful truth easily does without any confirmation or disproving on

the part of the real, while a truth held to be certain necessarily finds itself exposed to the creeping and obsessive desire for factual verification, for a victorious confrontation with the ordeal of the real. For this reason the man of doubt lets everyone remain in peace, while the man of certainty never stops until he has rung everybody's doorbell. The additional virtue of minimalist and uncertain discourse is thus to be inoffensive and not very compromising, to be unable to serve any cause, while an assured discourse can always be suspected of preparing some kind of crusade. To summarize: the "sureness" of a philosophical discourse, in the two senses of the term evoked earlier, resides in its simultaneously *critical* and *unusable* character.

If the principal aptitude of philosophy consists rather in denouncing errors than in enunciating truths, it follows—and this sounds paradoxical but is nonetheless true—that the major function of philosophy is less to learn than to *unlearn* how to think. Stupidity furnishes, moreover, a solid counterproof of this apparent paradox, since, contrary to what is generally and incorrectly thought, it consists not of a sloth of the mind but rather of a disordered debauchery of intellectual activity, as [Flaubert's] Bouvard and Pécuchet, those modern and indisputable heroes of idiocy, prove. Interest for "things of intelligence," as it is called in Offenbach's *La Belle Hélène,* is more often the mark of a mediocre mind than of a sharp mind. And it is certainly with some justice, and not just as an effect of coyness, that the most penetrating of French thinkers, Montaigne, declares that his mind is slow.

It is well known that the ordinary overestimation of the intellectual functions is such that if the majority of men in their madness fear to be considered impotent in the sexual domain, they fear at least as much to be counted as imbeciles—as if to reveal a lack of intelligence meant to lose all honor and almost to be scratched off the map of existence. Descartes clearly illustrates this universal desire for intelligence, as stubborn as it is absurd, and seems to detect no evil in it, in the entire first sentence of the *Discourse on the Method:* "Good sense is the most fairly distributed thing in the world; for everyone thinks himself so well supplied with it, that even those who are hardest to satisfy in every other way do not usually desire more of it than they already have" (7). I strongly suspect, for my part, that this inflation of purely intellectual values, obvious in all enterprises of radical separation be-

tween the body and the mind, is principally attributable to a megalo-
maniacal phantasm resulting from the need to cut the bridges between
the nature of the human being and the nature of every other thing, be it
animate or inanimate. Contemporary psychiatrists make of this mania
the nervous center of obsessional neuroses. This is a social climber's
phantasm, I would even say, the phantasm of someone who has indeed
raised himself above his animal origin by his intelligence, but who at
present must try to hide his descendance. I will also note that the
absurdity inherent in this will to intelligence consists above all in
granting more value to the representation of things than to the experience of these same things, to the ordeal of their tragic and jubilatory
intensity. To believe thus that the knowledge one can have of reality is
more important than the richness of reality itself is to chase after
shadows. There is indeed an ample species of false wise men who reach
peace in their souls only by means of a sort of general anesthesia
against the real which renders them incapable of fearing but also of
desiring—Paul Valéry, for example, who, moreover, makes no bones
about it: "I confess that I have made my mind into an idol, but I have
found no other." It would be impossible to express better the fact that
interest in intelligence is a translation of the incapacity to be interested
in anything, an incapacity which Bouvard and Pécuchet, before Valéry,
unhappily experience and which reminds us yet again of the subtle but
tenacious link which, for better or for worse, brings pure intelligence
into contact with absolute stupidity. One of Hergé's characters, Sér-
aphin Lampion, who incarnates total vulgarity, declares in *Les Bijoux
de la Castafiore:* "Understand that I am not against music, but,
frankly, during the day I prefer a good beer."[14] Impossible not to make
such a formula one's own (naturally on the condition that the word
"music" be replaced by the word "intelligence"), and Montaigne himself certainly would have adopted it when he declared in the *Defense
of Raymond Sebond* regarding "people of wisdom": "I esteem them
greatly, but I do not hold them in adoration."

It remains for me to explain how the principle of uncertainty is
connected to the cruelty principle, but the answer to this question is
self-evident. If uncertainty is cruel, it is because the need for certainty
is urgent and apparently indestructible for the majority of humankind.
Here one encounters a rather mysterious point of human nature, or

one that is at least yet to be elucidated: the intolerance for uncertainty, an intolerance such that it leads many people to suffer the worst and the most real of evils in exchange for the hope, vague as it may be, for the slightest certainty. Thus martyrs, uncertain as they are of establishing or even of defining the truth of whose certainty they are persuaded, are resigned to being *witnesses* to it—as the etymology of the word *martyr* indicates—by exhibiting their suffering: "I suffer, therefore I am right." As if the ordeal of suffering were sufficient to validate the thought, or rather the absence of thought, in whose name the martyrs/witnesses say they are ready to suffer and to die. This confusion about the cause for which they sacrifice themselves explains, moreover, the ever insatiable character of the expert in suffering (while it can happen that the expert in pleasure is fulfilled). Since no cause is truly within sight, no suffering will ever truly succeed in establishing it, no matter how long and hard one may be beaten. There is thus an ascending spiral in the cycle of punishment which is evoked somewhat comically by André Aymard and Jeannine Auboyer: "There is a psychology of martyrdom and it is eternal. . . . Thus there were volunteers for martyrdom, such as the Christians of Asia Minor, who under Commodus were so numerous in offering themselves to the proconsul that he turned them away after having pronounced several condemnations, recommending that they use ropes and cliffs."[15] One can only praise the liberality of this proconsul who, finding himself in a situation where he is unable to satisfy everyone, nevertheless consents by charity and within the means at his disposal to persecute at least a few of the supplicants.

The most disconcerting thing about the taste for certainty is its abstract, formal character, insensitive to what really exists as well as to what effectively can be painful and gratifying. Indeed, Nietzsche contrasts the richness of reality with the "poor" and "empty" character of certainty: " 'Grant me, ye gods, but one certainty,' runs Parmenides' prayer, 'and if it be but a log's breadth on which to lie, on which to ride upon the sea of uncertainty. Take away everything that comes-to-be, everything lush, colorful, blossoming, illusory, everything that charms and is alive. Take all these for yourselves and grant me but the one and only, poor empty certainty.' "[16] In the end, whether a certainty teaches us anything at all about the real is of little importance; it must only be

certain. This is why fanatic believers in some cause are recognizable
principally by the fact that they are ultimately totally indifferent to the
cause and are fascinated only by the fact that the cause appears to them
at a given moment, capable of being an object of certainty. A convinced
Marxist pays little attention to the theses set forth by Marx, a convinced
Stalinist little attention to the historical reality and psychology of Stalin.
What counts is the purely abstract idea that Marxism is true or that
Stalin was right, ideas that are quite independent of what Marx wrote or
what Stalin did. The adoration of a truth is thus always accompanied by
an indifference with respect to the context of that very truth. It sometimes happens that such fanatics, when they finally doubt their idol or
their successive idols, find peace only in a devotion to a humble but
indisputable cause—arithmetical truth, for instance. A person who has
believed in everything but also doubted everything can easily make an
excellent accounting expert at the end of his or her career; the verifying
of correct additions and exact accounts finally offers the occasion for an
indubitable and interminable pleasure in truth. Thus, according to Flau-
bert's project, Bouvard and Pécuchet, after having tried their hand at
everything, were to return to their initial jobs as scrupulous and irre-
proachable transcribers.

The pleasure in hurting people around oneself, often felt to be more
important than that of pleasing oneself, is perhaps the result of this
same idolatry of certainty. It comes from the confused idea that the
other will certainly feel a displeasure, while one is never quite sure of
the pleasure one could experience oneself.

The indifference of the fanatic with regard to his or her own fanaticism explains the apparently paradoxical fact that the stubbornness
displayed in upholding a cause is always accompanied by total versatil-
ity, that it is part of human credulity to be necessarily capricious and
fickle. Most of the time the act of faith is only a provisional compensa-
tion for the incapacity to believe and thus for the impossibility really to
distinguish the credulous from the incredulous or the fanatic from
the erratic. In short, every fanatic is a skeptic who is unhappy and
ashamed to be one. Or, stated otherwise, one is generally credulous
because one is incredulous, fanatic *because* one is erratic. Spinoza,
after Machiavelli and Hobbes, clearly notes this link between credulity
and the incapacity truly to believe, an incapacity which leads the credu-

lous person to pass perpetually from one object of belief to the next
without ever succeeding in finding satisfaction:

> This being the origin of superstition[17] . . . it clearly follows that all
> men are by nature liable to superstition. It also follows that supersti-
> tion, like all other instances of hallucination and frenzy, is bound to
> assume very varied and unstable forms, and that, finally, it is sus-
> tained only by hope, hatred, anger and deceit. For it arises not from
> reason but from emotion, and emotion of the most powerful kind.
> So men's readiness to fall victim to any kind of superstition makes it
> correspondingly difficult to persuade them to adhere to one and the
> same kind. Indeed, as the multitude remains ever at the same level of
> wretchedness, so it is never long contented, and is best pleased only
> with what is new and has not yet proved delusory.[18]

I shall note in closing that the taste for certainty is often associated
with a taste for servitude. This taste for servitude, very strange but also
universally observable ever since human beings began to exist and
began to think too much, I would say, to parody La Bruyère, can
probably be explained less by an incomprehensible propensity for servitude in itself than by the hope of gaining a little certainty obtained in
exchange for an admission of submission toward someone who declares that he will guarantee the truth (without offering, naturally, to
reveal anything about it.) Incapable of holding onto anything as certain, but equally incapable of accepting this uncertainty, people most
often prefer to defer to a master who affirms that his is the depository
of the truth to which they themselves have no access—Moses before
the Hebrews, Jacques Lacan before the faithful, the supposed son of
the prison guard before the prisoners (in aphorism 84 of Nietzsche's
Traveler and His Shadow [*Human, All Too Human,* 331)], or yet
another guardian, the one who watches over the law in the famous
Kafka parable and who accepts all the bribes without ever permitting
anyone to penetrate the secret, before the man of the provinces. Rather
than to assume their ignorance, they prefer to exchange their freedom
for the illusion that someone is there thinking for them who knows
what they cannot succeed in knowing. Belonging to a cause—that is,
fanaticism in all its forms—is thus less the work of the person who
rallies to the cause than of the intermediary and phantasmatic person
in whose name the rallying takes place. The fanatic himself does not

believe in anything; he believes instead in the person who in a muddled way he thinks believes in something. It is not I who believe, it is He; and that is why I believe in Him, although I know nothing of Him nor of what He knows. This belief by proxy says much about the nature of human credulity, recalling, if need be, that it results not from a natural propensity to believe but, on the contrary, from a total and intolerable personal incapacity to believe in anything.

3. Post Scriptum

The cruelty of reality is illustrated in a particularly spectacular and significant fashion in the cruelty of love, a well-known and already superabundantly analyzed theme, it is true. But it is the privilege of profound questions always to authorize a partially renewed analysis, as it is the privilege of any great work of art, a musical one, for example, always to offer material for a surprising interpretation which reveals heretofore unheard aspects and thus perpetually renews interest in the piece. Without claiming such a vast and daring ambition, however, I shall limit myself to relating the theme of cruelty in love to that of cruelty in general, to showing that the former is simply a variant—or "necessary variation," to remain within the musical metaphor—of the latter.

I take the term *love* here in its widest sense: love of another person, to be sure, but also and perhaps primarily love of life (or of reality), and finally love of self. I shall not speak of love of God, which would group together the three cases of love just cited (if one accepts the hypothesis of the existence of God), nor of the love of one's neighbor (abstract and unreal love—although often an agent of negative revelation of a very real hatred—which I disqualify because I have never found a trace of it elsewhere but in the novels of Tolstoy as well as in all examples of the literature of edification). It might be surprising to see love of things or love of self preferred to the love of a loved one, which would seem to contain the most acute expression of love if we were to believe the common sense approach, which moreover is absolutely right to assert this. One must distinguish, however, between the love which hurts the most—or which causes the most pleasure—immediately (love of a person) and the love which hurts the most and contains the most difficulties over the long haul (love of self, love of things). If it is true that the love of things is subordinate to the love of a person, it is also even more true that the love of a person is subordinate to the love of things, not for reasons of reciprocity but for reasons of hierarchical superiority. [Alfred de] Vigny is naturally accurate to write in two famous lines: "What importance has the day? What importance has the world? / I shall say they are beautiful when your eyes have said so."[19] The inverse formula would be of an even superior pertinence: I shall find your eyes beautiful if and only if I have first found the day and the world beautiful. In other words, assuredly nothing is as important and as gratifying in life as love in the normal sense of the word—nothing, if not *life itself*. This is what Spinoza expresses well when he defines love as "joy accompanied by an external cause." Love is only a variation—the principle variation, this is self-evident—of the love of life.

I would also add, in case it is necessary, that the cruelty of love of which I am speaking has little connection with the cruelty of eroticism as George Bataille understands it when he detects in carnal love (which is also and necessarily a little mental) the cruel project of physical destruction of the loved being, of an attack perpetrated against its "individuality." In other words, a will (manifestly inspired by Schopenhauer) to break the individual character to bring it back by force to the species of which it is only a figure, by proceeding to a sort of erotic deconstruction which begins with the kiss, first manifestation of the desire to bite, and finishes—if the amorous itinerary goes all the way to the end—with quartering and tearing to pieces. This is not the place to question the correctness or the falsity of this thesis (it shares a bit of both), but only to say that it does not directly enter into my subject.

To return to the cruelty of love (and to its relation with the cruelty of reality), I shall first of all make the observation that this cruelty is easily perceived at all levels and in all the accepted meanings of the word *love,* whether it is love of self, love of things, or love of a person. The paradox is that none of these objects of love is truly worthy of love, if one considers things coldly, and thus that every person in love, because he or she has always and necessarily made a bad choice, is condemned to venerate as the best what in reality is the worst and, moreover, what the lover soon recognizes as such—from whence the torture. "Odi et amo," says Catullus the poet, "Odi et amo. Quare id faciam, fortasse requiris. / Nescio, sed fieri sento et excrucior": "I hate and love at the same time. How is this possible? you shall perhaps ask. I do not know, but I say that this is the case and that I am crucified by it." This cruel observation is applicable to all forms of love. I love and detest myself, for I consist only of a project of total disappearance, carefully and craftily programmed, of a death for which I have received no grace, only a brief stay of execution. This is why the self is an object of hatred, as Pascal puts it. I love the things of the world and I detest them for the same reason: when it comes to duration, they are ultimately no better served than I. I love a person and I detest him, for he is inevitably destined to stop loving me (the cruelest, most vexing case for self-love), unless it is I myself who stop loving him. This is a less harsh but perhaps more sinister case, because it leads me to suspect that the origin of every disappointment resides in me (and not in the others), in my own incapacity to remain myself (to make my desire last, to stay the course, even to follow an idea). Chamfort summarized in a brief formula the terms of this alternative without issue: "Happiness is not an easy thing. It is very difficult to find it within ourselves, and it is impossible to find it elsewhere."

The cruelty of love (like that of reality) resides in the paradox or the contradiction which consists in loving without loving, affirming as lasting that which is ephemeral—paradox of which the most rudimentary vision would be to say that something simultaneously exists and does not exist. The essence of love is to claim to love forever but in reality to love only for a time. So the *truth* of love does not correspond to the *experience* of love. This is why the calming of the pain of a lost love also signifies an increase of this same pain, as Rousseau remarks in a passage of the *Nouvelle Héloïse*, since the end of love is precisely what is most cruel in love. One of Saint-Preux's friends believes he will calm Saint-Preux, who is plunged in a deep affliction, by making him see that every heartache wanes with time—to which Saint-Preux counters immediately and quite correctly that it only increases his pain to think that it will *end*. To forget one's suffering consequently means to reanimate the force of its cause, which may occasionally consist of the difficulty of loving a person and being loved by him, but essentially of the impossibility of loving anything. In the domain of love, the end of suffering is only the beginning of true punishment.

If love has sometimes been called a magician, in the sense that it casts spells upon people, as the title of a famous work by Manuel de Falla suggests, this is because it succeeds, or rather seems to succeed in accomplishing an impossible deed: to transform nothing into something, as well as to transform this same something into nothing in an inverse process. Plato was correct in the *Symposium* when he made love an ontological problem, the drunkenness of love an intoxicating sentiment of a fleeting contact with being. Love, like Janus, is a magician with a double and contrasting face: it knows how to make an object appear out of nothing by a trick of white magic, but also knows how to send it back to oblivion with a single wave of the wand by a trick of black magic. Manuel de Falla renders this magic well in a passage from *El Amor Brujo:* "Like a will-o'-the-wisp, love vanishes" (*se desvanece,* says the Spanish text of Martínez Sierra: disappears, evaporates, turns suddenly into nothing). Shakespeare's *Midsummer Night's Dream,* Marivaux's *Double Inconstance,* Mozart's *Così fan tutte* are other striking illustrations of this cruel evanescence of love, of its double power to appear and to disappear, to be and not to be. But, again, this ambiguity is none other than the ambiguity inherent in every species of reality.

I shall close with a remark that concerns love (in the usual sense) but has nothing to do with the thesis of this essay. Love is doubtless the most gratifying experience there is. It is, however, contrary to a tenacious preconception, never the occasion of a true "discovery." I mean that in love one experiments with something of which one always already possessed the notion—which explains the apparently paradoxical fact that so many thinkers have been able to speak so profoundly of love (Schopenhauer, Kierkegaard, or Nietzsche, for instance) without having known the real experience. It is the same for love as it is for the one hundred thalers evoked by Kant in *The Critique of Pure Reason:* those which are in my pocket have the inestimable advantage of existing and being mine, but differ in no way from the idea I had beforehand of those same thalers. This is also in a way what Freud expresses when he remarks that, given the resemblance between adult love and the infantile love for a mother, the supposed discovery of love is never anything but the occasion for a reacquaintance.

4. Post–Post Scriptum: The Nonobservable of the Real

In a scene from a Buster Keaton film, *The Three Ages,* we see a singular character, part astrologer, part meteorologist, deep in complicated calculations destined to determine what the weather is outside. Having decided that it is going to be a beautiful day, he engraves the information on a stone tablet (the scene is supposed to take place in ancient Rome) and goes out to post his result. Suddenly he returns inside, however, surprised by a snowstorm, and engraves a prediction of "heavy snow" which he posts straightaway, this time with no prior calculation whatsoever. Everyone naturally laughs at this charlatan's procedures. Upon reflection, however, the astrologer seems to me to demonstrate under the circumstances a remarkable freedom of spirit. He puts fact before opinion, and does so without a moment's hesitation.

Many others, probably the majority of people, if placed before a comparable dilemma, would choose the other path: they would prefer opinion to fact. If there is one human faculty that merits attention and appears prodigious, it is indeed the aptitude, particular to humankind alone, to resist all exterior information as soon as it does not fit the order of what is expected and desired, to ignore it if need be and as required. Ultimately, if reality persists, one will oppose it with a refusal of perception which interrupts all controversy and closes the debate— to the detriment of the real, naturally. This faculty of resistance to information has something fascinating and magical about it, at the limit of the unbelievable and the supernatural. It is impossible to conceive how an apparatus of perception goes about not perceiving, the eye not seeing, the ear not hearing. This faculty, or rather this anti-faculty, exists, however; it is even so common that anyone can observe it anytime at leisure.

Proust describes the virtues of this antiperceptive faculty quite nicely at the beginning of the *Recherche* when he analyzes the sentiments and reactions of his great-aunt in Combray with respect to Swann. The reader may recall that this great-aunt refuses to imagine that Swann, a friend of the family, also lives in a world of high society and artists, with no relation whatsoever to the society of Combray. The facts are stubborn, however, and seem to want to bring her ceaselessly back to a sentiment of reality, so numerous and eloquent are the signs which bear witness to the real position of Swann. Nevertheless, the great-aunt will never hear of such a thing, and it is marvelous to observe with what art—almost with what genius—she perverts the meaning of the information which comes to her day in and day out and succeeds in turning it to Swann's disadvantage. This is a game of messages sent which always ironically return to the sender. Message: someone informs the great-aunt that Swann possesses a famous collection of paintings. Reply of the great-aunt, addressing Swann: "Are you at least a connoisseur? I'm asking in your own interest because the art dealers are probably selling you really bad paintings."[20] Another message: she learns that Swann has dined "at the home of a princess." Reply: "Yes, a princess of the demimonde." Still another message: the family learns that Swann is an intimate friend of Mme de Villeparisis. Response from the great-aunt to her sister, who announces the startling news: "What? She knows Swann? And you claimed she was related to Marshall Mac-Mahon!" This last reply provides a good measure of the solidity of the wall which protects the great-aunt from all recognition of Swann's social status. It implies that every person forced to admit that he frequents Swann is immediately scratched off the list of high society. Before Swann makes the first step of progress in the esteem of the great-aunt, she will have reduced the entire European aristocracy to the level of commoners. This time it was Mme de Villeparisis, next time the Prince of Wales, the Count of Paris, and why not, if necessary, Marshall Mac-Mahon in person. Miracle of the antiperceptive faculty! One could show the great-aunt quite precisely all of the reality concerning Swann, but, thanks to the faculty, or because of it, she would nevertheless always be assured of *never* knowing anything about it. René Girard indeed comments on this point in *Deceit, Desire, and the Novel:* "The truth, like a bothersome fly, keeps settling on the great-aunt's nose only to be flicked away."[21] It is as if a bolt were pushed shut, which blocks all information and victoriously imposes an absence of perception of the most tangible and manifest evidence. Or as if an iron curtain were lowered which defeats reality, like the closing of a museum or a bar, which sends the late visitor out into the street unceremoniously: "Closing time, it's over, you must leave now." Wishing to defend its legitimate right to be perceived, reality would encounter the same failure as that of the visitor who would try to force his way into the museum or the bar: "I've already told you, we're closed." A striking example of this act of "closing" perception can be found at the end of a film which Joseph Mankiewicz adapted from a play by Tennessee Williams, *Suddenly Last Summer*. During the whole film Mrs. Venable fights against the true version of the facts which her niece and a doctor expose to her. Reduced to silence in the end by the weight of the evidence, she sends everyone away and returns to the upper floor of her house, disappearing in an interior elevator which isolates her from the world, and dismisses without appeal her interlocutors as well as reality in general. Tartuffe uses the same method, interrupting a confrontation which is becoming uncomfortable:

> Il est, monsieur, trois heures et demie;
> Certain devoir pieux me demande là-haut,
> Et vous m'excuserez de vous quitter sitôt.[22]

Thus, in certain circumstances an extraordinary security bolt deprives man of the normal use of his perceptive faculty (by man I naturally mean all persons, imputing differences of intelligence and perceptive sharpness not to the presence or the absence of the bolt but to the fact that the bolt is more or less closed). It is difficult, I know to understand precisely the nature of this bolt and the conditions under which it functions, and I would be tempted to say that whoever fully understood the lock's secret would understand the human person in its entirety. I would say only, and this is self-evident, that the bolt consists of the definition of a point beyond which one will perceive nothing, or to put it another way, and it means the same thing, of a truth which one decides once and for all to ignore completely. It marks the limits of a sacred territory (precisely like Proust's Combray). I shall also note that this bolt always has an *anticipated* character; it is a preexisting denegation of all critical investigation or later discovery, a sort of hallucinatory conjuration of the future, that is, of what is by nature eminently unpredictable and uncertain. One must introduce a nuance here and add that this conjuration is only half hallucinatory, since it shows itself to be effective, at least in a certain way. It is thus less a protection against present dangers than it is a "pre-caution," that is, an advance protection, an a priori refutation of future attacks. It is a necessarily contradictory refutation, since the dangers to come and the adequate protection measures will not be exactly known until later. Thus Abel Gance attempted to head off in advance every future objection leveled against his film *Napoleon* even before the filming began by solemnly declaring to the whole group of his collaborators in 1924: "I want to feel as I contemplate you a wave of force rising up that can sweep aside all the dikes of criticism." The mechanism of the bolt is recognizable here: I announce starting today that the film I want to produce is such that whoever criticizes it will be wrong. And if someone criticizes it later on, that person will simply prove what Gance was correct to announce in advance, namely, that it would be wrong to criticize the film. The bolt has slid shut and protects the filmmaker from everything just as it protects the great-aunt in Combray. In ancient Athens the procedure of *graphè paranomôn* forbade citizens, under threat of the strongest of sanctions—even death—from putting into question a law previously adopted by the assembly of the people. It offers a similar example of a bolt shut in advance.

What is most remarkable after all in the phenomenon of the refusal of perception is the fact that not only is the opinion sheltered by the bolt not invalidated by contradictory information and the stinging rebuttal which reality tirelessly brings against it, but, on the contrary, it is generally confirmed and reinforced by these very rebuttals. Just like systems made self-regulating by a feedback structure, the "refusal of perception" system is so well organized that its own miscalculations, far from weakening it, direct right back toward its own purposes all the energy resulting from its improper conclusions, its perpetual differences with the real. The mistakes it necessarily commits are programmed in such a way that they relentlessly feed the source of error which caused them in the first place, so that the refusal of perception is a system which not only produces errors but still further becomes fat and prospers from their presence. Let me invoke here a childhood memory of a student who had persuaded herself that our teacher secretly loved her, despite the sarcastic and often rather pointed words with which he cut off her every intervention. Each time she received such a rebuff in public, she never missed turning toward us with a triumphant look by which she seemed to be showing us how right she was and saying: "You see that I'm not dreaming—he loves me." I could also invoke Courteline's famous Boubouroche, whom a well-intentioned but badly inspired neighbor undertakes to persuade of the infidelity of his mistress. The ensuing story is well known. Boubouroche stumbles upon a rival for Adèle in his house, but quickly surmises a fidelity on the part of his mistress much greater than anything he had ever dared imagine. The feedback systems function here in an exemplary manner, leading Boubouroche to an unshakable conviction the maxim of which can be summarized more or less thus: "Adèle cannot be unfaithful to me. The proof? She is unfaithful." Naturally, Boubouroche was already certain of the fact, but now he has proof— and, after all, two certainties are worth more than one. The only guilty party in this whole affair is the prying neighbor, who will receive a severe reprimand. A reprimand well merited, for he should have known that all corrective information introduced into a system of "refusal of perception" is immediately transformed into a supplementary confirmation of which the sole effect is to bring to the mind of the nonperceiver that little bit of certainty which was still lacking.

Contrary to the commonly held opinion, the extraordinary power of resistance to perception which permits Boubouroche in Courteline or the great-aunt of Combray not to see what passes before their very eyes cannot be interpreted in terms of simple "stupidity." Such blindness is too close to what can easily be observed in manifestations of fanatic or hateful dementia to constitute a separate genus named stupidity, which would be defined as an innocent blindness, free from every suspicion of its participation in the neighboring genus of madness and hatred. One certainly can and even must speak of stupidity in the case of Boubouroche and of the great-aunt only if one adds, however, that this stupidity appears upon reflection to be indiscernible from what happens in the case of madness or hatred. True, good sense seems to oppose the idea of confusing in this way psychological manifestations which are reputed to be distinct from one another. But it is possible that good sense is wrong and distinguishes in a case where there is nothing to be distinguished, imagining, as Descartes would say, "formal distinctions" between objects which nothing permits us actually to distinguish. A more profound and exhaustive analysis, like the one that Leibniz's God would be able to bring to a conclusion, would perhaps ultimately demonstrate that the three notions of stupidity, meanness, and madness are three words designating one and the same psychological reality. I shall be satisfied here with a few brief remarks whose aim will be to show the fragility of the frontiers which have traditionally separated stupidity from madness on the one hand and stupidity from hatred on the other.

With respect to the first frontier, the one between madness and stupidity, I shall first note that madness and stupidity are like two natural allies which reciprocally aid each other as soon as a danger appears on the horizon—to such an extent that it seems to me hardly possible to grant the existence of one without simultaneously granting the existence of the other. No stupidity, if I can put it this way, can function by itself, with only its own forces to support it. When it decides that the reality offered to its perception is simply null and void, it requires the aid of the machine that ignores the real, that is, the talent which constitutes madness. And, reciprocally, no madness can function without the succor of a certain stupidity (nor, moreover, without the help of a certain dose of hatred), called to the rescue in case of an investigation which is too curious or a question which is too bothersome. Observing lunatics, whether they be truly insane or slightly neurotic, amply confirms this fact: as soon as he finds himself in serious difficulty, the mental patient unfailingly turns to an absurd justification or to imbecilic reasoning. Without the permanent help of stupidity, the exercise of madness would simply be impossible. The positions it occupies, being indefensible in themselves, would crumble under the weight of the first attack like so many houses of cards.

It is hardly necessary to show in addition that the wall behind which lunatics protect themselves from the real is of exactly the same nature as the one behind which every so-called normal but not so intelligent person, such as the great-aunt of Combray, protects himself or herself from realities the recognition of which could well bring disagreeable consequences. What Freud designates by the term "repression" is ultimately only a particular case of the bolt that can be observed in all "normal" cases of the refusal of perception. Freud makes the following remark in an article published in 1920: "The analysis went forward almost without any signs of resistance, the patient participating actively with her intellect, though absolutely tranquil emotionally. Once when I expounded to her a specially important part of the theory, one touching her nearly, she replied in an inimitable tone, 'How very interesting,' as though she were a *grande dame* being taken over a museum and glancing through her lorgnon at objects to which she was completely indifferent."²³ This refusal to perceive, this "non-perception" by which the patient triumphs so often and so easily over his or her analyst, irresistibly evokes the attitude of the great-aunt regarding Swann as well as that of Mrs. Venable bidding adieu to the doctor in *Suddenly Last Summer*, precisely at the moment when the doctor thought he had finally made a breakthrough. Decidedly, it is always the strongest who loses and the weakest who wins in this double game of madness and stupidity. In the end, there is no doubt that the one who wins here is weak, that he succeeds in undoing the forces of an adversary a good deal more solid than he is himself. Pierre Janet was most certainly perspicacious and profound when he attributed the general source of all madness to a deficiency of psychic energy. It must be added, however, that this debilitation is doubled by a very great force and that the energy which is missing from lunatics when they confront the real comes back to them increased as soon as it is a question of keeping the real, or whatever supposedly represents it, at a distance. This is why lunatics (and imbeciles for the same reasons) are simultaneously very weak and very strong. Very weak, being in no condition to bear the real. But also very strong, succeeding in their own fashion in effectively eliminating the real which afflicts them. And that force for eliminating the real is, I repeat, truly confounding. It is impossible to conceive of a counterforce which could ever effectively oppose such a power. One is thus necessarily led to ask oneself about the meaning and the value of whatever the treatment of neuroses might be, or what might be, furthermore, the intelligence and the competence of the psychiatrist or the psychoanalyst. Faced with such a solid front of madness and imbecility, the forces of a healthier or better-informed mind seem singularly derisory, and I would willingly venture to bet they will always lose.

An objection against this assimilation of stupidity and madness would be possible here, namely, the universal and justly recognized fact of extreme intelligence or sharpness which the majority of lunatics occasionally demonstrate. This objection does not hold, however, as soon as one understands that the set of strategic structures which can, it is true, mobilize a prodigious ruse and psychological penetration—one could even say at times a divination and clairvoyance, in the occult sense of the term—remain prisoners of the internal "truth" which must be sheltered from information arriving from the exterior, to such an extent that the intelligence of the lunatic, just like that of the imbecile, whose performances in this domain can be very remarkable, excellently serves the purpose of refutation but never the purpose of learning. More precisely, its paradoxical mission is to defend against intelligence itself. It is well known that the phenomenon of censure as it is practiced by collective ideologies and collectivist regimes obeys exactly the same causes and tends toward the very same objectives.

Indiscernible from madness, stupidity is just as indistinguishable from hatred. This association of stupidity and hatred seems to me so self-evident that I would consider underlining it to be a pointless gesture were it not for the singular and even rather surprising circumstance that most of the time it is not perceived. In fact, one can hear it said daily with respect to a person whose every deed and word are just so many manifest persecutions of those around him that he must not be blamed because he is, after all, we are assured, naturally excellent and fundamentally generous. It is simply that the person is slightly clumsy and does not realize what he is saying or doing. Here is an imaginary distinction between the deed of persecution and the supposed intention, between a stupidity responsible for the deeds and a goodness one could not hold responsible for the intentions, that does not stand up to the most superficial analysis. I would invoke here for the final time the example of the great-aunt of Combray and her perpetual refusal to perceive the social situation of Swann. One can—and indeed one must—interpret this refusal in terms of stupidity. But how not to interpret it as well in terms of jealousy and hatred? A reflection spoken by the great-aunt should suffice to enlighten the most well-disposed reader on this point. Evoking the princes of the French royal family, she declares to Swann: "People whom we shall never know, neither you nor I. And we get along very well without them, don't we?" (1, 18). It is impossible to summarize her hatred any better, as much with respect to Swann, whom she maintains at her own level with an iron hand ("neither you nor I"), as with respect to the princely family, whom she disdains in advance, knowing that a relationship with them is impossible ("And we get along very well without them, don't we?").

Pascal marvelously pokes fun at this illusory distinction between the deed and the intention when in the third *Provincial Letter* he contrasts the heretical deeds for which Arnauld is reproached, which everyone fundamentally agrees to be nonexistent, with his heretical intentions, the latter immense according to his detractors: "It is not the sentiments of M. Arnauld that are heretical; it is only his person. This is a personal heresy. He is not a heretic for anything he has said or written, but simply because he is M. Arnauld. This is all they have to say against him."[24] Here, naturally, the respective values of the deed and the intention are reversed. In the eyes of Arnauld's censors, the deeds and the spoken words are innocent but the intentions reprehensible; while in the case of the great-aunt, at least in the superficial opinion one can formulate about it, the deeds and the spoken words are reprehensible but the intentions innocent. The illusion is the same in both cases, however, for it obeys the same erroneous principle: a fallacious distinction between what one does and what one intends to do, between what one says and what one intends to say.

Notes

Introduction

1. Clément Rosset, *Logique du pire* (Paris: P.U.F., 1971), 70. Here and elsewhere in the introduction, the translations of the French texts I refer to are my own.
2. Jacques Bouveresse, *Rationalité et cynisme* (Paris: Minuit, 1984), 119.
3. Laurent-Michel Vacher, *Pour un matérialisme vulgaire* (Montreal: Les Herbes rouges, 1984), 172.
4. See Christian Ruby, *Le champ de bataille: post-moderne/néo-moderne* (Paris: Editions L'Harmattan, 1990), for a discussion of the characteristic aesthetic dimension of postmodernism.
5. Peter Sloterdijk, *Critique of Cynical Reason* (Minneapolis: University of Minnesota Press, 1987), 16.

Chapter 1

1. Henri de Montherlant, *Pitié pour les femmes* (Paris: Grasset, 1936), 167–68.
2. "The Man of the Crowd," in *Tales and Poems of Edgar Allan Poe* (New York: Scribner and Welford, 1885), 1:329.
3. Jules Michelet, *Le Peuple* (Paris: Flammarion, 1974), 70.
4. Benedict de Spinoza, *Ethics*, trans. W. H. White, in *Great Books of the Western World* (Chicago: Encyclopedia Britannica, 1952), 31:400.
5. The French word *jouissance* is difficult to render in English (as translators of Roland Barthes, for example, have discovered). It generally means pleasure of a sexual nature. Its etymological root is the same as that of *joie,* and Rosset plays on that relationship in this passage of his essay. (Editor's note)
6. Sigmund Freud, " 'Wild' Psycho-Analysis," in *The Standard Edition of the*

Complete Psychological Works of Sigmund Freud, ed. James Strachey (London: Hogarth Press, 1957), 11:223.

7. The French phrase "les hommes sont les 'semblables' les uns des autres" contains two ideas difficult to render together in English: (1) All men are created equal. (2) Every man is my fellow man. (Editor's note)
8. Homer, *The Odyssey,* trans. E. V. Rieu (Baltimore: Penguin Books, 1964), 184.
9. E. M. Cioran, *La Chute dans le temps* (Paris: Gallimard, 1964), 142.
10. Montaigne, *The Complete Essays of Montaigne,* trans. Donald Frame (Stanford: Stanford University Press, 1965), 852.
11. Arthur Schopenhauer, *Aphorismes sur la sagesse dans la vie,* ed. Richard Ross, trans. J.-A. Cantacuzène (Paris: P.U.F., 1964, 1964), 35.

Chapter 2

1. Maurice Blanchot, *L'Entretien infini* (Paris: Gallimard, 1969), 301.
2. Maurice Blanchot, "Nietzsche et l'écriture fragmentaire," in *La Nouvelle revue française,* 168 (1966), 967–83, and *La Nouvelle revue française,* 169 (1967), 19–32.
3. Martin Heidegger, *Nietzsche,* trans. Pierre Klossowski (Paris: Gallimard, 1971), 1:250.
4. Marcel Aymé, *Le Confort intellectuel* (Paris: Flammarion, 1949), 152.
5. Georges Bataille, *Sur Nietzsche: volonté de chance* (Paris: Gallimard, 1945).
6. Pierre Klossowski, *Nietzsche et le cercle vicieux* (Paris: Mercure de France, 1969).
7. Henri Birault, "De la béatitude chez Nietzsche," in *Nietzsche: Cahiers de Royaumont* (Paris: Minuit, 1967), 13–28.
8. *Nietzsche: Cahiers de Royaumont,* 13.
9. Friedrich Nietzsche, *The Gay Science,* trans. Walter Kaufmann (New York: Vintage Books, 1974), 223.
10. Friedrich Nietzsche, *Twilight of the Idols,* in *The Portable Nietzsche,* trans. Walter Kaufmann (New York: Penguin Books, 1954), 521.
11. Friedrich Nietzsche, *Beyond Good and Evil: Prelude to a Philosophy of the Future,* trans. Walter Kaufmann (New York: Vintage Books, 1966), 137.
12. Friedrich Nietzsche, *On the Genealogy of Morals and Ecce Homo,* trans. Walter Kaufmann (New York: Vintage Books, 1969), 218.
13. Nietzsche, *Human, All Too Human: A Book for Free Spirits,* trans. R. J. Hollingdale (Cambridge: Cambridge University Press, 1986), 213.
14. Friedrich Nietzsche, *The Birth of Tragedy and the Case of Wagner,* trans. Walter Kaufmann (New York: Random House, 1967), 158.
15. *Manuel de Falla* (Paris: Editions Cahiers d'art, 1930), 19.
16. Friedrich Nietzsche, *Thus Spoke Zarathustra,* in *The Portable Nietzsche,* ed. and trans. Walter Kaufmann (New York: Viking, 1982), 208.

17. E. M. Cioran, "Ébauches de vertige," *La Nouvelle revue française,* 318 (July 1979), 2.
18. Antoine Goléa.
19. Jacques Bourgeois.
20. The word *endroit* in Rosset's text is translated as "site" here. Rosset puts the French word in quotations and plays on its meaning by suggesting its compound nature: *en droit,* that is, the "right" of the real to be here present in the space described. (Editor's note)
21. Pierre Klossowski, *Un si funeste désir* (Paris: Gallimard, 1967), 193.
22. Nietzsche is alluding here to the operas of Rossini and Bellini.
23. Karl Schlecta, *Le Cas Nietzsche,* trans. A. Coeuroy (Paris: Gallimard, 1960), 27.
24. Johann Wolfgang von Goethe, *Faust,* trans. Bayard Taylor (New York: Random House, 1950), 16.
25. Gilles Deleuze, *Nietzsche et la philosophie* (Paris: P.U.F., 1962), 213.
26. Descartes, *Discourse on the Method,* in *Descartes: Philosophical Writings,* trans. Elizabeth Anscombe and Peter Thomas (Indianapolis: Bobbs-Merrill, 1971), 17–18.
27. Pierre Klossowski, "Circulus vitiosus," in *Nietzsche aujourd'hui?* (Paris: Union Générale d'Éditions, 1973), 1:94.
28. Rosset rewrites the expression *savoir-faire* (expertise, knowledge of how to do something) as *savoir-jouir* (knowledge of how to be joyful). (Editor's note)
29. Pierre Klossowski, "Oubli et anamnèse dans l'expérience vécue de l'éternel retour du Même," in *Nietzsche,* 227–35.
30. Gilles Deleuze, *Différence et répétition* (Paris: P.U.F., 1969).
31. Heidegger, *Nietzsche,* 1:201–366.
32. Roughly translatable as:

> They will return, the gods for whom you still weep!
> Time will bring back the order of the ancient days;
> The earth trembled beneath a prophetic wind . . .
>
> While the sibyl with the Latin face
> Is still asleep beneath the arch of Constantine
> —And nothing has disturbed that severe gate.

33. G. W. Leibniz, *Theodicy,* trans. E. M. Huggard (London: Routledge and Kegan Paul, 1951), 130.
34. Nietzsche, *Ecce homo,* in *Oeuvres philosophiques complètes,* ed. G. Colli and M. Montinari, trans. Jean-Claude Hémery (Paris: Gallimard, 1974), 8:248–49.
35. Friedrich Nietzsche, *The Antichrist,* in *The Portable Nietzsche,* 585.
36. Friedrich Nietzsche, *Dithyrambs of Dionysus,* trans. R. J. Hollingdale (Redding Ridge, Conn.: Black Swan Books, 1984), 67.
37. *La Volonté de puissance,* trans. G. Bianquis (Paris: Gallimard, 1947), 1:251.

Chapter 3

1. G. W. F. Hegel, *The Phenomenology of Mind,* trans. J. B. Baillie (New York: Harper and Row, 1967), 158–59.
2. *Pour un matérialisme vulgaire* (Montreal: Les Herbes Rouges, 1984), 149.
3. *Le Réel: traité de l'idiotie* (Paris: Minuit, 1977), and *L'Objet singulier* (Paris: Minuit, 1979). (Editor's note)
4. The French word for this meaning is *cru,* which comes directly from the Latin stem. (Editor's note)
5. Marcel Proust, *A la recherche du temps perdu,* ed. Jean-Yves Tadié (Paris: Gallimard, 1989), 4:3.
6. *Zibaldone,* trans. M. Orcel (Paris: Le temps qu'il fait, 1989), 91–92.
7. E. M. Cioran, *La Tentation d'exister* (Paris: Gallimard, 1956), 233.
8. Clément Rosset, *La Philosophie tragique* (Paris: P.U.F., 1960).
9. Jean-Jacques Rousseau, *Politics and the Arts: Letter to M. d'Alembert on the Theater,* trans. Allan Bloom (Ithaca, N.Y.: Cornell University Press, 1973), 32–33.
10. Immanuel Kant, *The Idea of a Universal History on a Cosmo-Political Plan,* trans. Thomas de Quincey (Minneapolis: Sociological Press, 1927), 4.
11. Samuel Butler, *The Way of All Flesh* (New York: E. P. Dutton, 1952), 317.
12. Montaigne, *In Defense of Raymond Sebond,* trans. Arthur H. Beattie (New York: Frederick Ungar, 1959), 57.
13. Samuel Butler, *Life and Habit* (London: A. C. Fifield, 1910), 1.
14. Hergé is the author of the series of Tintin adventures published in France. *Les Bijoux de la Castafiore (Castafiore's Jewels)* is one of the adventures in the series. (Editor's note)
15. André Aymard and Jeannine Auboyer, *Rome et son empire,* in *Histoire générale des civilisations,* ed. Maurice Crouzet (Paris: P.U.F., 1954), 2:373.
16. Friedrich Nietzsche, *Philosophy in the Tragic Age of the Greeks,* trans. Marianne Cowan (Chicago: Gateway Editions, 1962), 81.
17. That is, fear, or in Spinoza's philosophy the most general principle of retreat from the truth, a principle which corresponds more or less, it seems to me, to the principles of the retreat from reality of which I am speaking in this essay.
18. Baruch Spinoza, *Tractatus Theologico-Politicus,* ed. Brad S. Gregory, trans. Samuel Shirley (Leiden: E. J. Brill, 1989), 50.
19. "Que m'importe le jour? que m'importe le monde? / Je dirai qu'ils sont beaux quand tes yeux l'auront dit."
20. This example and the following ones are to be found in *A la recherche du temps perdu,* 1:16–21.
21. René Girard, *Deceit, Desire, and the Novel* (Baltimore, Md.: The Johns Hopkins University Press, 1965), 196.
22. Roughly:

Monsieur, it is three thirty;
A certain pious duty requires my presence upstairs,
And you will excuse me for leaving you so suddenly.

23. Sigmund Freud, "The Psychogenesis of a Case of Homosexuality in a Woman," in *The Standard Edition of the Complete Psychological Works of Sigmund Freud,* ed. James Strachey (London: Hogarth Press, 1955), 18:163.
24. Blaise Pascal, *The Provincial Letters,* trans. Thomas M'Crie, in *Great Books of the Western World* (Chicago: Encyclopedia Britannica, 1952), 33:18–19.

Index